A GUIDE TO DEVELOPING A SUCCESSFUL FAMILY AND NANNY RELATIONSHIP... YES, IT'S POSSIBLE

Alene Mathurin

Copyright © 2014 Alene Mathurin
All rights reserved.

ISBN-13: 9781497371224
ISBN-10: 1497371228
Library of Congress Control Number: 2014905232
CreateSpace Independent Publishing Platform
North Charleston, South Carolina

All labor that uplifts humanity has dignity and importance and should be undertaken with painstaking excellence and earth will pause to say, here lived a great street sweeper who did his job well.
—Martin Luther King, Jr.

Adhere to your purpose and you will soon feel as well as you ever did. On the contrary, if you falter, and give up, you will lose the power of keeping any resolution, and will regret it all your life.
—Abraham Lincoln

One person caring about another represents life's greatest value.
—Jim Rohn

For my son Elijah Gervais.

Your sweet smile makes my spirit come alive in me each day and seems to add a spark to the sun waking up the world around you.

For my nieces Davina and Daynia, dream beyond the stars.

I Love you!

TABLE OF CONTENTS

Introduction xiii
You're hiring a nanny. What should you look for? 1
Develop a good nanny contract 3
Understand your own unique caregiver's need 5
Nannies you also have a right to know who you are working for 6
Cultivating exceptional caregiver-family relationships 8
Trusting someone with your most prized possession…not any easy task 11
A nanny's attitude matters…What energies does a nanny take into the employer's home daily? 14
Everyone is entitled to fair pay for her work 16
Simple considerations and strategies to strengthen the family-nanny relationship.. 17
How to make it easier to work with a stay-at-home mom or dad......20
Hooray, we have finally reached a topic that may interest you or you may have personal knowledge and experience with: Overcoming everyday stereotypes people have about nannies......... 22
You are not a watchwoman. You are a nanny who gets involved in the child's activities. 27

Ways to get a child focused and engaged in an activity 29
Hello...yes...you, the one who always sits down in the
enrichment classes when the children might really need
your help. This might be a good read for you...Bookmark it! 31
How to resolve conflict among kids when caring for them 33
Nanny-parent conflict...how can it be resolved? 38
Working with twins 41
You can play an important role in getting older children used
to a new baby 43
When technology is too much for a young child 45
Don't burn the bridges you cross as a caregiver 47
Not all nannies are created equal 48
Never forget the reason you are in the home of your employer 50
Too much information: it's not anyone's business but your
employers' 52
Your personal meal preparation 54
You are the eyes and ears of the parents in their absence...act
like it 57
There's always something new to learn. Invest in your education
and find new training. 59
Avoid the dangerous practice of diagnosing the
children you care for 61
Playdate nightmares 62
Ethnic clinging in the nanny circle 65
Snacks, snacks, and more snacks 67
What's the importance of developing healthy sleep patterns in
young children? 69
Working with gay and lesbian couples 71
Common encounters a nanny may face when working
for same-sex couples 73
The "The Nanny Mafia," a seriously unproductive clan.
Refuse its membership 75

You are a live-in nanny and, like every woman and man, you
have sexual needs. What is a nanny to do in this situation? 77
Don't start what you can't finish. People are creatures of habit
and will pattern their lives based on your predictable schedule. 80
No one has the right to physically or verbally abuse you.................82
Emergency Action Plan 85
Dealing with the extended family while caregiving: the good,
the bad, and the dreaded grandma...88
Take time off for yourself 90
How do you deal with the mom with the "accessory babies"? 92
New addition to the family 94
I am not your superwoman…I get tired too....................................96
Dishonesty 98
Don't allow the ignorant acts or attitudes of employees
or management of the residential building where you work define
you as a nanny 99
A nanny is a nanny—not a cook, house manager, refrigerator
cleaner, clothes ironer, dog walker, or window washer.................. 101
Hello, mannies! 104
How do you work for a family that has a totally different value
system than your own? 107
The generosity of a family cannot always be measured in
dollars and cents 110
Perks on the Job 112
Regularly express appreciation. Say thank you............................. 113
If a family has had three or four nannies in one year, run.
Something is wrong! 115
A nanny is moving on. How can the parents and the nanny
make it easier for the children to cope? 117
Finding balance and tranquility in a job that could be
stressful, emotionally and physically..120
The dreaded Monday 123

What do you do as the caregiver when the child calls you
Mommy? 127
It's perfectly OK to say "No" to overtime hours 133
Be Organized, It will make caregiving less stressful......................135
"My child matters"…nannies whisper these three words
every day. 136
What happens sometimes at six in the evening when a parent
turns the key in the lock? Meltdown..138
Going on vacation and refusing to pay the nanny........................140
Working after hours...141
Be consistent with discipline in the presence or absence of
the parents...142
Be considerate when choosing enrichment classes for kids...........143
Phrases from nannies that make me say "Ouch" and should
never be used 144

PREFACE

A *Guide to Developing a Successful Family and Nanny Relationship* teaches, enlightens, and educates readers about the essential tools needed to maintain, sustain, and develop a long-lasting, healthy relationship within a family and caregiver dynamic. Its format, through which the pivotal everyday aspects of caregiving are covered by individual topics, along with occasional identifiable scenarios for families and caregivers alike, allows readers the ability to apply the lessons learned to their everyday lives with the goal of improving such relationships.

The purpose of this text is to remain objective and to understand that when the construct and fabric of a good family and nanny relationship deteriorates it may be the result of one or both parties violating a fundamental principle(s), which are the cornerstones of a successful relationship. The key to maintaining a successful family-caregiver relationship is ensuring harmony reigns in the home, resulting in well-adjusted, happy children.

As a mother I am especially moved by any situation that does not add value to a child's life, because kids deserve the most favorable home in which to thrive. As someone with significant experience as a caregiver and as a former caregiver recruiter, I have acquired pivotal information about familiar occurrences in the industry; however, I use this information in an ethical manner in the hopes of effecting positive change. As a professional life coach I understand the importance of aspiring to achieve a mutually respectful employer-employee relationship and how rewarding that relationship can be for the parties involved.

Therefore, the format of the book allows it to cover a wide scope of areas relating to caregiving, from positive interactions with children and extended family, meal preparations, intimacy, and so forth, to issues that may result in a breakdown of the caregiver-family relationship.

—Alene Mathurin, CPC

INTRODUCTION

A good caregiver is an integral part of a family. If the relationships within the family are healthy, a caregiver's presence could prove exceptionally rewarding for everyone involved, most importantly the children. The dynamics of a family-caregiver relationship vary from family to family, as the needs of families differ, but the foundation of a successful relationship begins with the understanding that everyone is equally important, despite the different roles they play. The caregiver must follow the rules set by the family, and that family should be sensitive to the caregiver's needs and private life. When this foundation breaks down, the construct of a good family-nanny relationship begins to fail. While each caregiver's ideal work environment will vary, general expectations include a relationship that is mutually respectful, with open communication and a pleasant work environment.

Attachment theory, which John Bowlby developed, states the earliest bonds formed between children and their caregivers have a tremendous impact throughout the life of that child. Hence, parents and caregivers must strive for continuity of care. Too often parents, instead of trying to resolve a conflict, simply fire the caregiver and hire the next available nanny. The unfortunate consequence is the child is bereft of that significant person and attachment. What is inevitable is the loss of this primary figure in the child's life causes the child stress, and the child becomes very weary of developing further attachments with other caregivers. This caution trickles down and hinders many facets of future relationships.

Similarly, nannies often simply find a different job, failing to air grievances they have with their employers, which ultimately leads to a lack of zeal in the daily execution of the nanny-job function. This behavior is not constructive and subsequently affects the most emotionally vulnerable in the household, the child.

*The cornerstone of a rewarding and sustained family-nanny relationship is mutual respect, effective communication, honesty, and integrity. However, maintaining effective boundaries is also crucial. Although the setting of the work relationship is extremely intimate, that is, within the confines of a sacred home, both the caregiver and the family can ensure healthy boundaries are created and maintained.

Ask important questions, such as how much of your personal life you want the caregiver to know and how much of her personal life do you want to know. It is very easy to share personal life stories, trials, and triumphs in such an intimate work relationship, but, before information is given freely, think about how this information may affect the long-term relationship. Would it add value to that relationship or could it be used destructively?

The nanny should not be privy to marital issues, financial woes, or your personal indulgences. Likewise, caregivers, the family should not be expected to listen to your mountain of problems, especially if they show no interest in your personal affairs. If you have a wild party the night before, keep it to yourself, as sharing it might make some families question whether you can execute your job. This does not add value to the relationship.

A Guide to Developing a Successful Family ...

Understand the goal in developing a successful family-nanny relationship is to ensure first that the children involved have the most stable and loving home in which to thrive; the family should also be left without anxiety as it relates to the caregiving aspect of their child's life. The caregiver should be excited to be at work. Finally, harmony must reign within the family unit.

YOU'RE HIRING A NANNY. WHAT SHOULD YOU LOOK FOR?

Hiring a nanny for your family is a delicate and intimate task that, when done right, can be extremely rewarding. However, when parents neglect important information, the process can become a nightmare that haunts every member of the family, especially the children.

In today's world, it's important to be detailed about hiring a nanny. Too often families leave out important issues, such as background screening, and rely instead on the pleasant smile and demeanor of a woman who shows up on time for an interview. Who was that agreeable individual? Who told you what an excellent employee she is? Was it the friend of the nanny being interviewed or someone her friend is employed with? Families must remain vigilant and be aware of the danger these trends hold.

You must perform a thorough background check on a potential nanny, including a national criminal background check, sex offender check, and DMV check. You should also obtain Social Security verification.

It is equally important you do not gather this information from online databases that often do not update their records frequently enough.

The norm with families is to interview a nanny and offer a start date that is within days of the initial interview. If time permits, offer the top candidates at least a week's trial period. During this time, you can observe interactions with your children as well as look for all the qualities that are important to you as a family.

Create an employee checklist to ensure the nanny's job description is explicit. It will come in handy during evaluation periods as well whenever you hear "That's not my job."

Stereotypes continue to be proven false with regards to which ethnic groups make the best nannies. Regardless of whether the nanny comes from a small Caribbean island, the countryside of Brazil, or a large city in Europe, what matters is she could be an addition to your family, and she brings with her values that promote an environment of growth for your children.

I am often asked "How do I get my nanny to stay with my family?" and I am lost for words. All individuals, regardless of economic status, cultural background, or gender, thrive when respect and care are shown toward them. Kind words, such as "You are performing well" or "The kids enjoyed the day at the museum with you," make a nanny feel appreciated.

I also encourage families, especially those using the services of a nanny for the first time, to hire a nanny consultant or coach to ensure important details are not left out during the initial hiring process.

Nanny coaches, who acclimate nannies on the job, will ease the parents' anxiety through their presence on the job for whatever period of time the parents choose.

Remember your home is a stage and the kids are your audience, eager to emulate what they see, which could be the both the positive and negative behaviors that are modeled; it is critically important to hire the right individual.

DEVELOP A GOOD NANNY CONTRACT

A nanny contract is a vitally important document. Imagine you have weathered and sifted through the storm of e-mails, discarding the creepiest responses to the nanny advertisements, and have met talented caregivers, and, frankly, some much less than talented. Perhaps you even needed to cut some interviews short because of their awkwardness. You have finally found the perfect candidate!

The objective now is to ensure all arrangements between you and the nanny are agreed upon and clearly understood. A written contract will serve as a point of reference for any issue that could arise. This contract serves as a guide for both the caregiver and the family, summarizing all they have agreed upon. This guide can help the household resolve or even prevent conflict. A good contract will include much more than the caregiver's job requirements and the degree of autonomy that a caregiver will enjoy. A good contract will facilitate harmony and cohesion.

The contract should include the following:

- *Hours of work, pay, and duties*

Everything related to compensation must be explicitly defined. How much pay will the nanny receive? Will that amount be paid weekly or bi-weekly? Will this salary take the form of cash, check, or direct deposit?

Work hours must be clearly spelled out and include provisions for overtime, holiday and sick pay, weekend pay, and any other payment arrangement. For example, will the nanny receive additional pay when she travels with the family? After all, the caregiver herself will likely incur additional costs during this time (e.g., her own childcare expenses).

The nanny and the family must also incorporate detailed information about vacations and vacation pay. Should the nanny's vacation be taken when the family takes theirs? Or is the nanny able to take whatever vacation time works best for her and her family? How much vacation time will she have?

- *Sick pay*

What happens if the nanny is out sick for two weeks? The contract should include a clause on sick pay that both the family and the caregiver agree on. *This is also a good time to determine the number of personal days the caregiver is entitled to apart from sick days.*

- *Probationary period*

A three-month probationary period can be useful, offering a set date where the family and the nanny can discuss the working environment and the caregiver's progress, or lack thereof.

Procedures for terminating the contract

During the probationary period, you may mutually agree to one week's notice of termination by either party. Then later, you may fall back on the standard two weeks' notice. Cause for immediate termination (where the family need not give the caregiver notice) should be agreed upon and outlined in the contract.

Although this process may be overwhelming to some parents, setting up a good nanny contract will help alleviate stress in the future.

UNDERSTAND YOUR OWN UNIQUE CAREGIVER'S NEED

Conflicts could be avoided if families determined and sustained the caregiver situation that works for them as a family unit. Parents comparing their caregiver situation with their friend's caregiver situation may be counterproductive. Admittedly, families hiring a caregiver for the first time may wish to bounce ideas off friends experienced with such hiring, but parents must be mindful not to emulate their friends' caregiving situations completely. One size does not fit all!

Every caregiving work situation is different, because each family is unique, as are the family's needs and the caregiver's responsibilities. Therefore, if a family has hired a caregiver, they need to independently decide on critical factors such as wage, vacation time, sick days, and all the myriad elements that can secure a healthy family-caregiver relationship or not. The advice of other families should remain just that, advice that will help a family objectively map out their own caregiving situation.

NANNIES YOU ALSO HAVE A RIGHT TO KNOW WHO YOU ARE WORKING FOR

A nanny interviewing for a job with a family needs to compile some basic information about the hiring family that will help her determine her compatibility with the family and, thus, the job position. Never take anything at face value, and get some information about the family, such as the parents' places of employment, membership affiliations, and at least a contact or reference who can shed some insight on who the potential hiring family is.

The majority of people who hire a nanny will conduct a thorough background check to know about the individual who will be with their vulnerable children. The importance of conducting an in-depth background check and motor vehicular check on the potential nanny cannot be fully stated.

Nannies must likewise be proactive in finding details about potential employers to ensure their safety. This information gathering is in no way a sign of disrespect to the hiring family. On the contrary, it should signal the potential employee is sound minded and meticulous in decision making and could be an indication of what type of employee she may be.

Information gathering about the family can be executed in several ways, including getting a contact number from nannies who have been employed by the family in the past and the names of two business associates who can give character references about the family. This is important for many reasons, including the need to weed out families who might have had problems with nannies in the past, such as failing to fully compensate them, continually giving returned checks, or violating fundamental issues like respect and boundaries. The more information you can get, the better your chances of ensuring that you don't accept a job with employers with emotional or psychological issues, employers with their own prejudices, or those who may be difficult to work with. Doormen are great resource people and will, in most cases, give insights into who the families may be.

The more questions you ask during the interview process, the more likely you are to get an insight into their personalities and the way the family functions as a unit. Ask questions about the kids, their temperaments, and their reward and correction systems. Listen as the family outlines the job description, and compare it with the compensation, the number of kids, and the hours of work, and make a sound judgment as to how realistic and fair it is. This will shed light on the potential employers' thoughts and expectations.

Look for clues that tell you more about the family. Did they ask anything about you as an individual or about your children? This may be an indication of whether they are self-centered, selfish individuals whose only concern is their own family and not anything that pertains to you.

If a family has had several nannies over the past few weeks, or even months, then grab your pocketbook and focus on the door. There's something wrong with that picture, and most times, it's the people facing you in the interview.

CULTIVATING EXCEPTIONAL CAREGIVER-FAMILY RELATIONSHIPS

Cultivating a strong family-caregiver dynamic can induce longevity and success. This is one of the key ingredients in ensuring the household is run smoothly, and the children, parents, and caregiver are in harmony. If either the family or caregiver neglects this important aspect of the relationship, discord will emerge.

To contribute to such harmony, you will need some tools to ensure a strong foundation and cohesion.

- Respect: Respect is an integral component of any successful relationship, allowing for ideas to be articulated and questions to be asked and validated by both parties. Ultimately, when a family respects the caregiver and vice versa, a caregiver is able to bounce ideas about childcare off the family. The family is thus able to respect these ideas, adopt them if necessary, or respectfully disagree while simultaneously validating the caregiver's ideas. In the same way, a caregiver, no matter how seasoned, must be able to learn from a first-time mother or father about childcare issues or even job execution. Respect opens the door to trust, which communicates one believes in the other's ability to make a good judgment call. Building respect requires a fundamental caring for the other person. It requires both the caregiver and the family being aware of each other's feelings and being sensitive and respectful of those feelings. True respect stems from viewing the other party as an equal rather than as a subordinate.

- Communication: As humans, no matter what type of relationship, we have a deep desire and need to be able to freely express feelings and to be listened to. This is no different in a family-caregiver relationship. If both parties are able to freely and respectfully express themselves, finding solutions, easing tensions, and ensuring cohesiveness as it relates to rules and job functions will follow. The ability to freely communicate suggestions and feelings allows both parties to feel respected and like a valued member of the team. On the contrary, if any one of the team members feels whatever he or she is trying to bring to focus is falling on deaf or preoccupied ears, resentment and the harboring of feelings detrimental to a family-caregiver relationship will emerge. The actual execution of daily childcare needs is already too physically, psychologically, and emotionally demanding to fail to listen to grievances.
- Goals and job Description: A well-defined job description and goals help employees remain aware of what expectations you have for them and leave little room for employees to hide behind the excuses. A family needs to formulate clearly defined job terms, roles, and responsibilities in order for a caregiver to work as efficiently as possible.

Caregivers must be able to be self-starters, which simply mean if a routine situation changes at the spur of the moment, they are able to think critically and act quickly and confidently to ensure the well-being of the children.

Families and caregivers need to meet quarterly for the caregiver to be evaluated based on his or her performance, discuss ways to achieve better results, provide rewards and incentives for increased performance, and discuss ways to make the home the most pleasurable place for everyone involved, especially the children.

- Integrity, honesty and trust: Integrity, honesty, and trust are essential to achieving a successful relationship between the caregiver and the family. If any of these ingredients wither, that decline causes the family-caregiver relationship to atrophy.

Children emulate any behavior that is modelled in the home. Hence, when basic human dignities and values are violated and disrespected by anyone, the children learn this too. The home is the first performance stage for children. Thus, the people who they trust the most, parents and caregivers, must be cognizant of the "performances" they are putting on in the household.

TRUSTING SOMEONE WITH YOUR MOST PRIZED POSSESSION...NOT ANY EASY TASK

Often people see caregivers with a child they care for, and, because of the number of caregivers in major cities, many assume that it's easy for parents to give over care of their children to someone else. But, in fact, this is an emotionally daunting task for parents. So how can a parent negotiate the emotional transition necessary in entrusting his or her child to a nanny?

A smooth, semi-painless transition begins with hiring the right individual. But first you must understand and identify your unique family needs. Are you looking for a live-in or live-out nanny? Will the job be a full-time or part-time job? Are you looking for a nanny who can provide early childhood education or someone flexible enough to travel with the family? A family needs to ask and resolve many such important questions before placing an advertisement for a nanny or beginning the interview process.

A smooth, semi-painless transition also involves understanding the individual who is being hired to care for the children. This first comprises of an extensive interview with the caregiver to ensure compatibility with the hiring family as it relates to values, rules, expectations, and work ethic. Ensure conflicts do not exist in values, as such conflicts can spur problems later.

Then a family must take all the necessary time to dialogue with the caregiver's references and leave no stones unturned, no important questions unanswered, which will offer the family insight about that individual.

I strongly recommend an in-depth background check, which will alert the family to any known criminal activities or driving violations. A comprehensive background check is better than the basic background check sold online, as the latter does not give as much detail. Although the comprehensive check is far more involved and expensive, it is worth every dime, because the safety and well-being of a child should never be compromised.

Also ensure that the caregiver is certified in pediatric and infant CPR. These classes are available at most Red Cross locations.

You should give the potential caregiver a period to acclimate. This probationary period could also be used to observe behavior, the way the caregiver executes various tasks, her overall rapport with the child, and, subsequently, her work ethic. If the family does not have the time because of work constraints to supervise the new caregiver, I highly recommend hiring a professional nanny coach who will be the eyes and ears of the family while they are at work. It helps alleviate normal anxieties a family will experience when a new caregiver is hired. The success of hiring a nanny coach stems from the fact that this individual will not only work within the confines of the home but also accompany the caregiver to the child's classes, to the playground, or on playdates.

A skilled coach can ensure recommendations are made about childcare services offered by the caregiver and will look for early warning signs from the caregiver, which could indicate potential problems. Investing in a nanny cam also helps monitor what is being done in a home and ensure the well-being and safety of a child is never compromised or violated.

Most parents rely on the support of other friends who are parents and have been able to successfully integrate a caregiver into their household. In most cases, these parents organize playdates and activities where the new caregiver is able to spend time with a trusted family, most times, a stay-at-home mother and her caregiver. The family could give the parents constructive, nonjudgmental feedback on that caregiver. Finally, as cliché as it may sound, listen to your gut instincts. If the potential caregiver's actions or words set off an internal alarm, you owe it to yourself and your children to pay attention to it. Be mindful also of well-intentioned caregivers who may be nervous during an interview and make some mistakes. If you recognize this and are still not comfortable, feel free to request a second or third interview.

A NANNY'S ATTITUDE MATTERS... WHAT ENERGIES DOES A NANNY TAKE INTO THE EMPLOYER'S HOME DAILY?

With many families' schedules and time stretched thin, the increased stress of their jobs and the demands of running a household, who needs another negative Lucy around, especially in the comforts of a private dwelling? Nannies, be mindful of the conscious or unconscious energies you are taking into your employer's home. An effective caregiver understands the importance of not allowing their personal stresses to govern their actions and attitudes while working.

Clearly understand that a positive and optimistic person can be like a ray of sunshine in the home and may help quell existing tensions. Likewise a caregiver who is seemingly always upset, never smiles, and has little to say can make the relationship with employers very awkward and difficult.

Simple gestures like a genuine smile, a warm greeting, a calm demeanor, and a positive outlook can go a long way, and eventually your employers will associate you with feeling good. This is paramount in a successful relationship.

❦ Families, also be mindful not to allow your own personal stress affect your relationship with your caregiver. If an individual is stressed, that person's tolerance level is lower, and he or she may be quick to negatively react to a situation that may not have warranted that approach. Take a "time out" and reflect on the problem you have with the caregiver, and approach it with the goal of improving the work situation.

EVERYONE IS ENTITLED TO FAIR PAY FOR HER WORK

While running a small nanny agency, I often came across nannies who were seeking employment, because the family they had worked with previously refused to fully compensate them for their services. It was difficult for me to believe these complaints initially! This was simply *not* possible. Ultimately, the sheer number of complaints shook me out of my slumber.

Non-compensation is indeed an issue within the industry. Although the intimate setting of a home-based workplace sometimes camouflages the actual professional who offers the services, that intimacy does not condone this very inappropriate breach of law. If a family employing a caregiver suffers a financial setback, and is thus unable to compensate the caregiver, the moral course of action is to assist that caregiver in finding another job and providing unbiased, truthful references. Many caregivers live from paycheck to paycheck. They cannot just wait while the family sorts out their financial situation.

SIMPLE CONSIDERATIONS AND STRATEGIES TO STRENGTHEN THE FAMILY-NANNY RELATIONSHIP

A good caregiver is tough to find. If you locate one, do all you can to keep her. Some childcare experts recommend a weekly parent-caregiver meeting. This promises parents insight on the children's development, while simultaneously allowing parents to discuss the caregiver's job functions, share concerns, and celebrate achievements. This family-nanny weekly dialogue should be done not only to air grievances but also to brainstorm other ways of effectively handling tricky situations. This will ideally serve as a learning opportunity for both parties. The caregiver likely handles different situations in a certain manner for a reason, and the parents, if desired, can provide alternatives.

Even better, open weekly dialogues can offer working parents fresh insight and perspective on their children's behavior, social skills, and temperament, as well as any other areas of concern the caregiver may have. This can help parents reconsider their parenting style. The caregiver, on the other hand, should give a detailed account of the children's activities and weekly progress.

Following the terms of your employment contract with the caregiver is one of the best ways to avoid future conflicts. If your contract with the caregiver reflects an agreement where she's entitled to two weeks' vacation time, which she is able to take independent of the family's own vacation, do not refuse to pay her when that time comes because she is using her vacation time and you must pay an additional caregiver in the absence of your contracted nanny. Do not ask the nanny to work late week after week unless she has requested additional work hours. Even if you are paying the caregiver an attractive overtime pay scale, over extended periods, her free time will become more valuable to her than the additional money earned. She may even become disgruntled if you repeatedly arrive home later than expected or call her a few hours before her designated leave time to inquire if she can work late. She may have her own childcare time restrictions or other activities to which she has committed, such as going to the gym or school.

Another point of contention can arise when the nanny gives you a not-so-favorable report about your children's behavior, attitude, and/or respect for authority. Parents, if you do not follow through with consequences for your children's misbehavior, your children will likely learn that the nanny's reports are meaningless, as they will face no undesirable results. This lack of assertiveness and swift action in dealing with children who violate the family's set rules teaches them that they are not obliged to follow the nanny's instructions while in her care and will weaken the nanny's position in your household. This could be considered offensive to the caregiver and could cause the family-caregiver relationship to decline.

Understanding the caregiver's personality and using common, practical, and fair approaches in dealing with your nanny will pave the way toward building a successful relationship. Inevitably, the family and the caregiver will sometimes disagree; however, such disagreement should be a learning opportunity for both parties, as well as a way to improve the dynamics of relationship over time. No relationship is perfectly harmonious, but respect must always be paramount. Parents, ensure you model routine, intentional, and effective communication and conflict resolution strategies within the household.

To build a potentially permanent trusting family-nanny relationship, parents, you must deal with unavoidable conflicts quickly and fairly. Ensure that conflicts are dealt with immediately to avoid compounding them with situations that occurred previously. Remember that such conflict resolution is geared toward improving a workable situation and guaranteeing continued harmony in the home. Ensure that both you the parents and the caregiver use effective communication skills to detail grievances, avoiding foul language and being mindful of your tone. Display a positive, productive attitude.

The goal of conflict resolution is to improve a bad situation within the household, ensuring continuity in your childcare regimen and harmony in the household.

HOW TO MAKE IT EASIER TO WORK WITH A STAY-AT-HOME MOM OR DAD

I can hear you saying "I don't think so," or "I think I'll pass on that job." It's not as bad as some caregivers make it out to be. In today's technological world, more parents have the option to work from home. As a parent myself, I applaud them.

The presence of Mom or Dad should not interfere with your task at hand. I understand having a parent at home can lead to new squabbles, because children behave differently when a parent is around. Children who are normally well behaved when you are alone with them can suddenly become more defiant, because a parent is present, and will throw tantrums to illicit a reaction. This too can be worked out as long as the caregiver and parent(s) have harmony as it relates to rules, boundaries, and matters of discipline.

The parent must explain to the child that when the caregiver is on duty, the caregiver is in charge and only liaises with the parent if necessary. This approach helps the child understand the hierarchy in the household. There must be a concerted team effort and cohesiveness in setting rules that create consistency and clarity for the children, which may limit the number of times a child bangs on the parent's office door.

Another concern of many caregivers is the feeling of always being under the parents' microscopes; hence, they feel that they must tread cautiously when executing their daily task and caring for the kids. This problem, too, has a solution. In order to avoid this uncomfortable situation, articulate your concerns to your employers and, in turn, validate any concerns they may have.

In a caregiver-family relationship, both parties must be able to accept constructive criticism to improve the work situation. The parents must understand and allow you breaks while the children nap and time to check in on your own kids, so you do not feel the need to hide when you these things. *Never work for anyone who does not acknowledge the importance of your own family.*

Lastly, don't believe there is a monster behind the closed office door without clear, valid, and objective reasons. Caregivers often fail to understand their employers and, consequently, make judgments that are not warranted. Take time to understand your employers' likes and dislikes and respect them. Do not expect them to be who you want them to be. Employers are individuals with their own ideologies.

Of course, when you know for a fact there *is* a monster behind that closed office door, start looking for new opportunities.

HOORAY, WE HAVE FINALLY REACHED A TOPIC THAT MAY INTEREST YOU OR YOU MAY HAVE PERSONAL KNOWLEDGE AND EXPERIENCE WITH: OVERCOMING EVERYDAY STEREOTYPES PEOPLE HAVE ABOUT NANNIES.

If you ask average people what they think a nanny's job is, the majority will respond that it is caring for children, changing diapers, and pushing children in a stroller. While there's truth to that, most people do not recognize the nanny's role extends far beyond the custodial care of kids or the important contribution a good nanny makes in the American home and society.

Nannies indirectly ensure Wall Street is open, because they're the ones who relieve the CEOs, the executives, the brokers, the doctors, and the teachers from their parental duties, so they can perform their professional ones. In many situations, nannies work at live-in jobs, so their suburban employers can get to the metropolitan cities on time to work.

While a few bad apples in the nanny world have made it difficult for some people to see the meaningful contribution these hard-working multitaskers, fight separators, friends, confidants, playmates and cooks make, we can't underestimate their importance to families. You might be shocked how many times a day nannies have to prove they are not the illiterate, uneducated people some people make them out to be. Take a minute to laugh as you see what Jane, a smart nanny who is also a full-time college student, is about to face.

Jane is walking down Madison Avenue in the early morning rush in New York, pushing an almost two-thousand-dollar Bugaboo double stroller with two precious kids. As she hurries along to the kids' expensive "Jump and Roll" class, she encounters several different people, most of them smiling.

Not too far into her trip, she meets "The Bodyguard," who intentionally stops Jane to express her disgust at the caregiver's negligence in leaving the house without ensuring that the kids have hats and mittens on, as it is cold outside. What "The Bodyguard" doesn't know is that the happy children in Jane's stroller refuse to wear hats and mittens, and the parents have no qualms about it. Jane wouldn't have a problem with the adult showing concern for the kids, but "The Bodyguard" spoke to her in a supercilious and condescending manner.

It's Friday, so Jane is happier than usual and ignores "The Bodyguard" and presses on. Not too far off she meets "Mr. Don't Have A Damn Clue" who tries to strike up a conversation with her. With two now-screaming kids in the stroller, she ignores him and continues on her journey, rushing to make it in time for the children's class.

Instead of understanding this was the wrong time to approach a woman for a date, he rants with offensive language at her with the intention to inflict emotional harm. Jane would have had a few choice words for "Mr. Don't Have a Damn Clue," but she's a smart nanny who respects the kids she cares for and knows she's an important role model in their lives, so she presses on.

I'm sure you have your own stories of the times you were made to feel less of who you are because of some people's stereotypes about your job. Those stereotypes come from people who see the nanny's job as unchallenging and reserved for the illiterate immigrant or the uneducated woman.

Nannies make no apologies for the fact that they wipe little noses, separate children and mediate fights, push all types of strollers, and clean up little "tooshies," but, for many, they wouldn't trade their roles for anything. They know it takes smart women to sometimes work up to twelve-hour shifts, doing a fantastic job of juggling and caring for occasionally two, three, and even four kids at a time, and then handing the kids back to their parents every night.

I have numerous years of experience nurturing and caring for children and have enjoyed every bit of this experience. I have celebrated wonderful milestones in the kids' lives that I was part of, like the first few steps, first words, first days at school, and countless treasured moments that are irreplaceable.

Only a clever and industrious multitasker, after a long day of work, is able to prepare meals for her own kids, ensure their homework is done, and read bedtime stories, before crashing into a deep sleep because of the day's exhausting and demanding activities. Like everyone, the nanny has a life beyond her work. She may be a wife, a partner, a mother, a friend, and a student, and her worth is not measured by the job she does or what one perceives the importance of the job to be.

I feel obligated to share my own story of how an uneducated fool tried to humiliate me when I was a nanny in New York City. I had my treasured companion, a double Mountain Buggy stroller at my side, with the two most adorable girls one could imagine buckled inside. The girls were exhausted from the playground and ballet class, so I decided to stop at an upscale store to pick up a necklace set I'd been eyeing for several weeks.

As I entered the store, I made immediate eye contact with one of the attendants who looked at me like I was an intruder. My little friends in the stroller weren't crying, so we had not disturbed the peace of the other shoppers. I quickly maneuvered the agile stroller between the aisles, trying to get another attendant to help me, but no one seemed to care that I needed help, and I felt totally invisible in the not-so crowded room.

I finally asked an attendant to get my beautiful piece out of the case, but she quickly shouted, "They're not on sale today." Did I ask the impolite lady for the sale item of the day? No. I wanted that piece of jewelry, and I was able to afford it. It constantly called my name, and I wasn't ready to ignore that call.

After that woman tried to get me out of the store by saying they had no sale, I became the center of attention for some of the shoppers. Their looks seemed to say "You don't belong here. You should be pushing the stroller outside or playing at the park." I had done all that. I was well within the family's rules of what I could do with the kids I cared for, and I was able to spend two hundred dollars on a piece of cosmetic jewelry, so why was I made to feel like an intruder?

I had to teach this woman a lesson about her misgivings about the nanny. With my dignity intact, I left the store, knowing I would be back later with a mission.

After work, I made my way up Fifth Avenue and headed to that store, still bruised from the treatment I had received earlier. I was no longer dressed in slacks; I had changed my clothing and now blended with the other shoppers.

Why was that woman smiling so pleasantly at me now? Had she forgotten me so quickly? Because I didn't forget her! Not only did she treat me badly, because she thought I was less of a person because of my job, but she should have known that you never mess with a woman who wants a beautiful shoe or piece of jewelry. Why was she asking to help me now?

I asked for her manager and articulated my disgust for the treatment I had received earlier. The attendant had a blank stare on her face when she heard the sound, educated argument I made about her misgivings toward me. Did she expect me to be unable to communicate or stand my ground because I was *only* a nanny?

I knew she worked on a commission basis, so I grabbed a handsome attendant and allowed him to sell me the piece I wanted. She stared as I pulled out my card and paid for my item. What a fool she had been to judge me or treat me with disregard because I was a nanny.

I was sure of two things: I wouldn't return to shop at that store again, and the store attendant would think twice before treating another nanny badly.

YOU ARE NOT A WATCHWOMAN. YOU ARE A NANNY WHO GETS INVOLVED IN THE CHILD'S ACTIVITIES.

Get up, sit on the floor, role-play, dance, and sing if you have to. But get involved!

Childcare shouldn't be limited to, or confused with, mere custodial care, which involves ensuring the children are safe, feeding them, wiping little noses, and changing diapers. There's more to childcare than that. Children deserve well-rounded caregivers who are spontaneous with engaging activities and are also quick thinkers in case of unforeseen emergencies. Nannies should recognize the important role and responsibility entrusted in them at such a pivotal time in the young children's development.

Research shows that toddlers who are psychologically stimulated perform better in school, are more confident emotionally, and are better at articulating their feelings. Therefore their overall care should not only include custodial care but also age-appropriate activities and play that will socially, cognitively, and psychologically help the children.

Playtime is "child discovery" time. It's a time when you can learn important details about children. Who are their "imaginary friends," what characters do these "friends" have, are their feelings hurt, and what needs are they articulating while they are playing? Most of the time, children's imaginary friends are simply mirrors of what's going on with the children. Listen to what they are saying, as this is a good way of getting the information needed to correct a behavior or overcome a fear or anxiety.

WAYS TO GET A CHILD FOCUSED AND ENGAGED IN AN ACTIVITY

Over the course of many years of caregiving I've learned that to get a child involved or interested in an activity, the adult sometimes has to take the role of a playmate. There's nothing more rewarding to a child than when a caring adult joins in playtime. It's supercool to any child when you put on the superhero cape or tutu and your princess voice while engaging in playtime.

Depending on the child's age, level of concentration, and even developmental stage, activities such as reading, coloring, and role-playing may be great ways to engage a child. However, be mindful to consider how tired the child may be or duration of these activities in order for them to be effective. While some young children are able to sit and listen to a short story, with other children, you may be lucky if you get three pages read.

One effective way of getting a child's attention is to read using a friendly, young child's voice and descriptive gestures to bring the story and characters to life. Cuddling on a sofa or lying next to the child on a mat is also effective. A favorite stuffed animal or toy is comforting and creates an atmosphere of relaxation, which is needed during story time.

Be consistent with when you read, either right before afternoon nap for those kids who still nap or before bedtime. Whatever time of day, make it fun for the child. Let toddlers and preschoolers choose the book, and, when there are multiple children, allow them to take turns choosing the books.

HELLO...YES...YOU, THE ONE WHO ALWAYS SITS DOWN IN THE ENRICHMENT CLASSES WHEN THE CHILDREN MIGHT REALLY NEED YOUR HELP. THIS MIGHT BE A GOOD READ FOR YOU... BOOKMARK IT!

OK, nannies, the parents have researched, found, and paid for expensive enrichment classes for their kids, and you have the task of taking them to those classes. Most of the classes, especially those for toddlers, need parental or caregiver involvement to ensure the kids really benefit from them. So my question now is... "Why are you sitting in the corner of the classroom playing on your telephone?"

Children are more prone to emulating behavior and learning from people they trust. When you hold their hands while they paint or try a new dance move, they will not only respond faster, but they may also end up enjoying the activity more because of your participation. It also fosters a sense of security for the child who is around many new faces.

On the other hand, if your little one is having a meltdown at a class, throwing a tantrum that may disrupt the class or upset the other children, the only polite thing to do is excuse the two of you from the class and give the child some time to calm down. This also teaches an important life lesson of being mindful of other people.

So jump and roll in a tumble class, paint, draw, dance, and have fun with the kids you care for. That's the whole idea of caring for little people. Regardless of the activity, the process of creating is much more important than the end result. So applaud and congratulate the work, even when the art work may be barely recognizable.

HOW TO RESOLVE CONFLICT AMONG KIDS WHEN CARING FOR THEM

No two children are the same; likewise, no two conflicts are the same. However, there are some guidelines you can follow when trying to resolve conflict.

Rule One: Understand what the conflict is.

You cannot resolve a conflict and teach appropriate behavior when you do not understand the reason for the conflict.

Caregivers often tell children they have no reason to cry, which is certainly not true. The children may not be physically but emotionally hurt. They are sometimes unable to articulate their feelings and control their behavior because they are overstimulated, physically exhausted, or believe their caregivers will not validate their feelings. This leads to inappropriate behavior. Effective caregivers take time to listen to the children they care for and correct the behavior based on the situation at hand.

Rule Two: Validate the child's feelings.

Everyone loves to be heard, especially children. It may be difficult when children are screaming out, toys are being thrown across a room, or little heads are banged on a surface or the floor. Your initial reaction is essential if the conflict is to be successfully resolved.

Simply remove the children from the situation and ask them to exchange crying for words and explain to you what bothers them. Not only does this new environment capture the child's interest, it also may make the problem less immediate, allowing the child to articulate the actual problem. While they try to explain their feelings, use phrases such as "I'm sorry you feel that way," or "I'm sorry that your feelings are hurt," to give the child the confidence that someone cares and listens to whatever is going on. This teaches young children how to begin a dialogue in conflict resolution.

Rule Three: Know the kids well enough to see when a conflict is imminent.

Reading cues from the children may help eliminate a total meltdown or a conflict with a sibling or playmate. As a caregiver who is aware of the children's tendencies and patterns, you know, for example, that a child is possessive about a certain toy, such as Lego bricks, regardless of who it belongs to. Even though there are five hundred bricks, the child "has to have" the blue one that a playmate has. The old adage "The grass is greener on the other side" is fitting. The toy a child is playing with loses its novelty as soon as another child has a different toy or game.

When you are tuned in with a child's behavior patterns, you can avoid conflict by developing quick responses based on the situation. Knowing the child you care for does not like sharing the Lego table, designate yourself as the distributor of Lego pieces, and ensure you compliment each child's creation. Not only are you involved in the child's activity, but you also indirectly teach the valuable lesson of being part of a team and working together, thus avoiding a possible meltdown because someone refuses to share.

Distract young children when they are doing something that's inappropriate, remove them from an unsafe situation, and model the appropriate or correct behavior. Toddlers and infants do not understand right from wrong and depend on you to keep them safe. At this young age they are like sponges and will absorb, emulate, and learn behavior patterns from the people they trust. It's paramount caregivers are cognizant of this fact and make every effort possible to model the right behaviors and values.

Rule Four: If children are tired, hungry, anxious, or overstimulated, they will likely cry.

Children and toddlers who don't get sufficient rest are more likely to throw tantrums and behave inappropriately. As a qualified caregiver, it's important for you to understand when a child has had enough physical activities, play, and stimulation. Not understanding this sets the stage for tantrums, crying sessions, and total meltdowns.

A caregiver should be able to read cues from children and know when they've had enough. Allowing the children to have either a downtime or nap calms them down and refocuses their attention. Be consistent with nap times, downtimes, and waking schedules. As much as I'm a big proponent of treks to the playground, museum, and parks, it is equally essential that children receive adequate rest and that those times are well balanced. Not only do rest periods rejuvenate children, but they are also good for their mental and physical development.

Rule Five: Choose effective, age-appropriate, parent-approved discipline, and be consistent with it.

If children understand there are consequences for inappropriate behavior, they will still test the limits, but there is a greater probability they will behave appropriately. Rules have to be clearly defined and articulated so the children understand.

When the rules are broken, a caregiver must enforce whatever discipline method follows the parents' approved guidelines. For some families, it may mean a time out; for others, it may mean losing a favorite toy; and for older kids, it may mean losing a privilege.

When possible, find ways to help the child correct the behavior. For instance, if a child hurts someone's feelings, the child should apologize. If a child makes a mess, the child should clean it up or be part of the clean-up process.

Discipline should always be consistent, performed at the time of the inappropriate behavior, and done with clarity, so children understand why they are being corrected. Discipline should be done without anger, inappropriate language, or screaming in order to be effective. Children mirror behavior from the adults in their lives, especially the ones they trust; therefore, a caregiver has a huge responsibility in acting appropriately around them.

The objective of discipline is to teach children acceptable behavior; therefore, whenever possible, teach rather than punish. Use positive affirmation and recognize the children's efforts as much as you would their failures. For every negative recognition try to recognize at least three positive ones to help build the child's self-esteem. *No* caregiver is allowed to hit a child, no matter what the situation.

Rule Six: Reward good behavior.

It's easy to recognize unacceptable behavior, but a caregiver should always compliment positive behaviors as well. Children love compliments and feeling like they are pleasing the people they love. Pointing out positive behavior and finding an effective reward system encourages that behavior. Rewards, such as baking cookies with older children or earning a star on a display board in the home, give a child a sense of pride. The visual display encourages the child to earn more rewards and thus the recognized good behavior.

Using positive reinforcement language, such as "I'm so proud of you," "I knew you could do it," or "You are awesome," help nurture that positive behavior.

Rule Seven: Maintain calm, positive, assertive energy.

To be able to effectively resolve or handle conflict, a caregiver has to remain calm and in control of the situation. Unnecessary shouting in no way quells a situation; in fact, it adds to the level of chaos that may be present. Shouting at children only makes them more nervous and exacerbates a bad situation.

NANNY-PARENT CONFLICT...HOW CAN IT BE RESOLVED?

Every relationship has problems and the nanny-parent relationship is not immune to disagreements, conflicts, or gray areas that could frustrate both parties. What should set an alarm bell off is when that relationship becomes a continually contentious situation where there's a lack of respect and healthy family, and employee boundaries are violated. Coming from different cultural, social, or economic backgrounds, people have differing views about how things are to be done in childcare, and this must be respected.

Nannies, even though you may disagree with the way your employers parent, you must take your cues from them, unless the situation may endanger the child or yourself. There are too many instances of nannies who brag about their invaluable years of service and the undeniable expertise they have developed along the way but refuse to acknowledge that some parents may do things differently from what they have been doing on other jobs, resulting in continued conflict. This becomes the perfect recipe for an even more stressful work situation.

To avoid conflict, look for common ground with the parents and embrace those similarities rather than the differences.

Likewise, parents, be prepared to listen to your nannies, as this sends the message you value their feedback and, when you disagree with the nannies' suggestions, ensure you are not condescending. The common phrase "It's not what you say, but how you say it" couldn't be truer than in this situation.

There are also times when heated arguments between parents and caregivers occur, and the exchanges are sometimes hard to digest. What's really shocking is that some of those arguments are about things two mature individuals could talk about, but the employers seem to feel the need to remind the nannies that it's their kids, their home, and their rules, rather than that they are a team with one goal, which is the well-being of the kids.

When parents open their homes to caregivers they must show respect by at least hearing them out or considering their points of view. Never forget that children model the behavior of the ones they trust.

Respect is the fundamental basis of a good family-nanny relationship, and it creates a healthy environment for the children where they will learn to respect others. The way you handle conflict as responsible people in their lives will set the stage for them to learn how they can also resolve their conflicts.

When a caregiver-family relationship gets to the point where there's always a shouting match, or one or both parties are verbally or emotionally disrespected, then it's the perfect time to sever ties.

We have seen a lot of horrible situations where children have become victims of frustrated and angry caregivers, and there's no justification for this. Parents, you must look for warning signs and take the action that's in the best interest of your children. There are also situations where good caregivers have been physically, emotionally, and psychologically violated, and you should also know when it is time to move on.

Nannies, a job is not the place to show what a strong-willed individual you are or how intolerant you are. It's not the place to showcase your argumentative skills. It is, however, a place where you can impact the lives of children in a positive manner by modeling the right behavior and help create a happy and stable environment for them so they can feel secure.

On the other hand, you will encounter difficult employers. Evaluate the situation and, if it's not healthy, move on to a more compatible family.

WORKING WITH TWINS

Double the work but also double the fun is a good way of looking at the care of twins. Imagine two babies crying at the same time, because they are hungry, tired, wet, or simply need cuddling. You're strapping one in the stroller or car seat while the other screams. Caring for one child is a daunting task, so how do these hardworking parents and caregivers care for two? There are simple, straightforward techniques that make caring for multiples easier and less stressful.

First, ensure routines and schedules are precise. This includes nap times, meal times, and diaper changes. There will be days when you'll be sitting in a safe place, with one child lying on your knees while you're burping another. When caring for twins, I often took refuge on the floor, because it was much safer.

Avoid the pitfall of getting the newborns used to being held constantly. If they can only be comforted by being held, a nightmare scenario may develop later when both babies cry to be held at the same time. If you know everything is all right and the babies are safe, it's perfectly fine if they cry occasionally.

Although you may be the queen of multitasking, you may not be able complete basic child-centered household chores on some days. You shouldn't be afraid to tell your employers the overall care of the children takes precedence over the care of the house, if that's part of your job responsibilities. A good employer with sound judgment will understand and respect that.

As the children get older, take time to get to know them as individuals. Although they are twins, their personalities, likes, and dislikes are unique. While it's easy to refer to them as "the twins," get into the habit of calling them by their names and help them build their sense of self as well as their unique individualities.

Wherever there are kids, there will be competition, rivalry, and conflict; however, as the caregiver, avoid making comparisons between the twins and never create competition between them. Recognize their individual strengths and nurture them, using positive reinforcement to improve skills that may be lacking.

Some children are needier than others, and there's a natural tendency for the needy child to demand all the attention. As an effective caregiver, make a concerted effort to ensure each child enjoys valuable alone time or comfort time with you. Ensure one child doesn't get all the attention while the other is left alone. Phrases, such as "We take turns," help older children understand they are both being considered.

Don't be afraid to ask for a break when you know you've had enough, especially if you work night shifts, have a live-in job, or put in extended hours. It's just as hard for you as it is for the parents, so they should understand. You are no good to the kids if you are chronically fatigued.

YOU CAN PLAY AN IMPORTANT ROLE IN GETTING OLDER CHILDREN USED TO A NEW BABY

There's a new baby in the family, and suddenly the older kids you care for won't do anything you ask them to do. They seem angry and throw frequent tantrums. They suddenly lose their independence, can't communicate feelings, and become needy.

Don't be alarmed by this behavior, but try to see the situation from the children's perspectives. In their minds, someone has treaded on their territory and taken their parents' and caregivers' attention, and everyone is talking about this new baby. They may be hearing phrases they're not used to, or don't want to hear, such as "You're big kids now," "I'm not able to attend to you now," or "I'm busy helping the baby." Young children might perceive these phrases to mean the newborn is more important to the family. The children will do what it takes to regain the lost attention, including throwing tantrums, being defiant and, in some cases, showing hostility to everyone, including the newborn.

The question now is how do you, as a caregiver, ease the transition for the children and make it less stressful? Make a concerted effort to have one-on-one time with the older children, so they don't feel they have to compete for attention with the newborn. While the newborn is napping or having downtime, get involved in activities such as coloring, painting, dress-up sessions, and block games.

Make the older children feel part of the newborn's care, perhaps by allowing them to get a new diaper, dispose of a used diaper, or hold the infant's bottle while you supervise. Catch phrases, such as "I could not do it without your help," give children a sense of satisfaction and pride and make them feel a part of the day-to-day care of the infant. It's difficult for young children to accept a newborn as part of the family if they feel isolated from the baby's care.

During this adjustment period young kids are more likely to seek negative attention and break every rule they know. As much as it's important to show empathy and validate their feelings, it's equally important to remind them of family rules and boundaries. Remind them, without nagging, that breaking the rules has consequences. Use positive reinforcement to encourage good behavior, and correct unacceptable behavior instantly, so it does not become habitual.

If you work for a stay-at-home mom, suggest she spend time alone with each of the older children while you care for the newborn, and encourage her to engage in activities like going to a class, park, or playdate with them.

WHEN TECHNOLOGY IS TOO MUCH FOR A YOUNG CHILD

Bookmark this page and grab a pen and paper. You've got an assignment.

That was fast!

Let's take an inventory of all the gadgets that are available to the child you care for, especially the ones that lead to instant temper tantrums when they are taken away.

---

iPad	iPod touch	cell phone
television	computer	video games
Wii	Xbox	PSP

OK, just listing these gadgets exhausts me, but don't say that to the little ones you care for. Given the chance, this new generation of children would likely spend every minute they were allowed playing with these gadgets.

Rules pertaining to the use of electronic devices, the time allocated to their use, and the type of games allowed are at the sole discretion of the parents and take precedence over your personal beliefs.

There are interactive educational games that can help children with problem-solving skills, reading, and spelling, so I don't believe all video games are harmful to kids. It's a question of how much time kids play those games and what type of games they play. We don't need research to tell us what the result will be if children don't get adequate exercise, which could be a result of the amount of time spent playing games or watching television.

When parents take time to ensure that their children understand the limits and rules for the use of those technological gadgets, you must ensure the kids follow those rules, and there should be no compromise without the consensus of the parents. While kids will test the set boundaries and rules, they depend on you to help them follow the rules in the absence of their parents.

Sadly, some caregivers use those gadgets as a way to calm down a child who is throwing a tantrum or as a way to avoid messy art projects or treks to the neighborhood park. This simply reflects laziness and a lack of creativity. Research suggests kids who are closed in a room playing games fall behind their peers in social and communication skills and perform at lower standard such as reading and writing. Research also suggests kids who play video games have faster reaction times, which can be beneficial for certain aspects of learning. What we have are lots of pros and cons for children being exposed to computers, video games, and television.

I believe everything just requires a healthy balance. So enjoy summer mornings at the parks and playgrounds, get involved in new art projects, enjoy the snow with the kids in the backyard in the winter months, visit the libraries and take advantage of the creative, age-appropriate activities they offer. Then, during the time the family has allotted to free or downtime, allow the kids to enjoy whatever medium the family has approved.

DON'T BURN THE BRIDGES YOU CROSS AS A CAREGIVER

When trying to transition from one family to another family as a nanny, good, verifiable references that validate your work ethics and highlight your strengths and skills are important. Undeniably, not all jobs will end on good terms but, whenever possible, ensure you perform your tasks to the best of your ability. You'll need those references when another family shows interest in hiring you.

NOT ALL NANNIES ARE CREATED EQUAL

Honda and Bentley both make cars, but the two cars are very different. The same is true of nannies and caregivers. Therefore, their salaries, benefits, and other perks depend on several factors, including skill sets, experience, job descriptions, and the family's finances. It's a dangerous practice for nannies to compare salaries, as this may lead to conflicts within nanny and parent circles.

The saying you get what you bargain for can't be truer than in this situation. When negotiating a job, ensure the compensation equates to your skills and the contribution you make to the children and family. Be mindful to include yearly salary increases, bonuses, and commuting and food expenses. Discuss overtime, weekend, and holiday pay as well as a taxi allowance when you work late at night.

For nannies who travel overseas with families, there should be a salary adjustment for working outside of your home base and for the extra hours worked. If you are flying out or taking a cruise with the family, discuss important matters like insurance, accommodations, and meal allowances, and factor in any expenses you may incur as a result of your absence from your own children, such as additional childcare expenses. A sensitive and caring family will also be mindful of the safety and well-being of your children while working away with them.

Even when a family may not be able to pay a top-notch salary, the rewards of working for one who appreciates your work far exceeds a high salary with a family where you're not comfortable and may be treated with disrespect and disregard.

NEVER FORGET THE REASON YOU ARE IN THE HOME OF YOUR EMPLOYER.

You're not a mediator in the family's squabbles or a contributor to the family's contentious saga.

If you work in such an intimate setting as a family's home, at one point or another, you'll undoubtedly hear and see fights, heated arguments, in-law quandaries, and much more. It's no different than in your own home where you also have bickering among your children, spouse, and in-laws.

What's different in this case is you are at this particular home to help ensure the children receive the best possible care and are truly content. You are a professional and an employee who knows how to ensure healthy boundaries are always maintained at the workplace.

In a situation where the parents are having a heated disagreement and the kids are present, take the kids to the backyard to play, or suggest an impromptu visit to a playground or park.

You have no business hauling news about one spouse to the other; this just creates, or adds to, existing conflicts. Whatever inappropriate behavior you see, leave to the spouses to handle, as long as it doesn't involve you or affect the children you care for. It's no business of yours if Mr. Smith, your employer who works from home, is constantly having friendly chats with Janice, who conveniently visits only when Mrs. Smith is not home or is away on a business trip.

Your business is to ensure that while the kids are in your care, they are not exposed to the inappropriate activity or negligent behavior of a parent. This can be done by simply removing them from the situation when it's warranted.

We all know the in-laws will visit, and the mother-in-law may not like her daughter-in-law, and vice versa, or the mother-in-law may think the son-in-law is too fat or not wealthy enough. We've heard it all. However, it's not your place to strike up gossip about your employers when the in-laws visit. Don't allow cheap gossip to be the basis of your relationship with the in-laws and extended family members. You're not their courier of news events that happen in the family you are employed by.

Find engaging things to talk about with the children's extended family, whether it is grandma, grandpa, aunts, or uncles. Fill them in on the children's developmental progress and the funny things they say, or show them the art projects they've missed out on.

Whatever you do, *stay quiet* about the family's private affairs. It's not your business, and it's certainly not the business of the extended family if they weren't filled in by the family in the first place.

TOO MUCH INFORMATION: IT'S NOT ANYONE'S BUSINESS BUT YOUR EMPLOYERS'

My employer just bought a pair of shoes that cost one thousand dollars, and she already has so many of them. She leaves all her soiled clothing on the floor in her room and expects I will pick them up. This is the cheap chatter you may hear in some nanny circles, which is uninteresting, not stimulating, and doesn't fulfill any purpose. This is simple gossip.

When nannies get involved in this type of behavior, they may not be doing something they should be doing, like engaging children in activities, being occupied with the kids at the playground, or helping a child in the playroom figure out how a toy works.

What happens in your employers' home should stay in the employers' home. Taking their personal information and sharing it with others violates their privacy. Employers who hire you to work in their homes trust you, and it's a disservice to them when this trust is desecrated. It may be the perfect recipe for good, juicy gossip, but the average, busy, fair-minded nanny with an interesting life of her own doesn't want to know how your employer stays skinny, where the family vacations, what their Hampton residence cost, or the number of cars they own.

This type of cheap rhetoric is so common and monotonous that those listening want to scream out "Enough." Don't be a gossip, and if you are, I trust you now know you might be a nuisance to some of your peers.

YOUR PERSONAL MEAL PREPARATION

Especially if you are one of my Caribbean sisters, you may understand that in our part of the world, the spices, flavors, and aroma of our food are as rich and plentiful as our sunshine. When prepared right, our varied dishes, from *oils downs* to *bacalao,* will have anyone coming for seconds, even the skinny ones.

However, estate homes, elite apartments, and expensive Hampton homes where windows are adorned with costly draperies, are the wrong places to prepare *bacalao, mondongo,* curry goat, and fried fish. Leave your exotic cooking for the weekends or evenings in your private residence. What you consider a pleasant aroma might be repulsive and dreadful to others.

Humorous corner:

Janice had just settled in Southampton on Long Island, New York, in the private residence of her new employers. She'd worked there for about two weeks as a live-in nanny. The home was spacious and beautiful, and no one would imagine there were three-year-old triplets in the house. The old Victorian home was like the ones Janice had seen on television, with huge windows and expensive wall paintings everywhere. Her employers seemed kind so far, and the children were adjusting well to her.

The only problem was the type of food she had been eating. Cold-cut sandwiches with bland soup were certainly not what she was used to. She knew she had to bring some "real" food back to that house if she was to survive on the job another week.

On Monday afternoon she quickly unwrapped some codfish she had brought back from Brooklyn and hurried to prepare it while the children napped. Her employer worked from home and spent most of her time on the top floor in a small, cozy office that seemed almost like a hideout. As the codfish boiled, Janice tidied up some of the children's toys in the playroom.

"Janice, Janice." Mrs. Shakles's voice came screaming across the room.

Janice looked up, wondering for a second how this loud sound could come from such a tiny person. Before she could answer, Mrs. Shakles was right in front of her, inquiring about what she called the "pungent odor" in the house.

"I'm just preparing my lunch," Janice replied casually.

Before she could say anything else, her employer was in the kitchen with her hand covering her nose, looking inside the pan with an amazed look on her face. You would think that she had just seen a ghost, when all that was in the pot was codfish, a few green bananas, and some lentils; true island food like Janice would say.

"I have a business meeting in a few minutes," Mrs. Shakles said as she frantically sprayed the room with air freshener.

Luckily, the lunch meeting was late, and the smell of codfish had time to dissipate.

"I think you are a wonderful employee," Mrs. Shakles told Janice, "But this type of food should be cooked while you are at home. I'm sure it tastes really good, but that smell is agonizing, to say the least."

Dear Mrs. Shakles, you can take a Caribbean woman out of the Caribbean, but you can't take her spices and the authenticity and uniqueness of her cuisine away from her.

Dear nannies, what you might think looks and smells good, someone else may have a different opinion about. Hold off on the codfish until you get back home.

YOU ARE THE EYES AND EARS OF THE PARENTS IN THEIR ABSENCE...ACT LIKE IT

Parents rely on you to give them feedback about their kids on a day-to-day basis. This helps them enjoy any milestones the child may have achieved in their absence. Your feedback also helps them become aware of any issues, including behavior, medical, or social problems that may need to be monitored and corrected. It may be the child's social interaction with other children at playdates, in the playroom, or at a class. As we all know and agree, kids act differently in the absence or presence of their parents.

In today's world of technology and the easy access to a camera, which most basic phones are equipped with, it's easy to share pictures or a short video clip of the child. It may be that the child takes a few steps, begins to crawl, or stands up for the first time. The parents would welcome and be thankful for your kind thought.

Exercise good judgment when you update parents about the kids' days or when you give them other pertinent information. Don't compete with a screaming child who's excited that Mom is home from work and eager to tell her what happened that day.

As long as it relates to the well-being and care of a child, there's no such thing as giving too much information to the parents. Parents should incur some of the cost of text and phone calls, especially if they communicate frequently by phone with the caregiver.

THERE'S ALWAYS SOMETHING NEW TO LEARN. INVEST IN YOUR EDUCATION AND FIND NEW TRAINING.

There are lots of classes for nannies and caregivers available at colleges and through online resource centers and institutions, including the International Nanny Association (INA).

The INA has an exam that is available to all experienced nannies. A passing grade helps demonstrate the nanny's knowledge as it relates to certain aspects of the job functions and responsibilities. Upon successful completion of the exam, a nanny receives an INA credential exam certificate, which may help a nanny gain employment in highly sought-after nanny jobs. The INA credential exam certificate is the only nanny credential that is nationally recognized. For more information on this exam, visit the INA at www.nanny.org.

Private institutions and organizations also offer programs and training that cover topics such as nutrition, child development, childcare, safety, and family dynamics. Enrichment classes can help sharpen skills and educate nannies about new techniques and findings as they relate to their areas of expertise. The cost and length of these programs vary according to the institutions providing them. A nanny who's highly skilled and well trained is easily differentiated from the average babysitter and can negotiate higher wages and benefits.

Research now provides us with a wealth of information that supports the theory that infants require more than just basic nurturing, like hugs and cuddles, in their early developmental stages. While I fully understand and support the importance of cuddles and hugs, we now know if children are to grow to their full potential, they must also receive developmentally appropriate social, physical, cognitive, gross motor, and emotional stimulation. This kind and level of care is most often given by caregivers who have undergone training in various aspects of caregiving.

AVOID THE DANGEROUS PRACTICE OF DIAGNOSING THE CHILDREN YOU CARE FOR

I've often cringed in disbelief as caregivers give their reasons for why children act out or behave inappropriately. They may label kids with ADD, autism, or ADHD. Only qualified, accredited professionals can diagnose childhood disorders.

It's a disfavor to the kids to start labeling them with disorders on your own. Other caregivers within the child's circle may also begin to treat that child differently and may pass along the ill-informed and unsupported information to other parents.

I've worked with children who possess certain tendencies and behavior issues; however, that does not mean they have a disorder. Avoid making a judgment of the child's condition. Instead, point out tendencies to the parents and leave it up to them to discuss any issues with the child's physician who will refer them to any necessary specialists. Be sensitive to the family and children by ensuring you do not label a child with one particular disorder or another.

PLAYDATE NIGHTMARES

If you understand "the toddler's law of property," you will be able to see when fights are imminent and can avoid some unpleasant experiences in a playroom or on a playdate. The writer of the toddler's property law clearly captured the mind-set of a young child.

Children, however, need to learn when they are young the importance of respecting others, taking turns, sharing, and working together as a team. Whether it's at the Lego table or in the plastic tunnel, children get opportunities to learn fundamental skills that will benefit them later in life. It's almost impossible to avoid conflict among children but, as a caregiver, you must do everything possible to reiterate important values such as no hitting, no biting, no scratching—simple, keep-your-hands-to-yourself rules—when kids play.

Once those rules are broken, there should be a set of consequences that will deter the kids from that type of behavior. Those deterrents should have the support of the parents and must be age-appropriate and articulated well enough that the kids understand them.

Most playdates are either hosted at a child's house or in a playroom or other public space, like a park, playground, or enrichment center.

Perceptions of playdates differ from one parent to another. There are parents who simply want their children to socialize and have fun with their peers, while other parents want total nanny involvement in whatever activity the child does while on a playdate. Regardless of parent expectations, a playdate is a chance for a caregiver to monitor the children's social development, recognize whether there are social impediments that may need addressing, and give children the time and space to fully explore their independence. This, of course, is based on the age of the child.

The nanny's involvement should not be to the point that children aren't given the chance to perform simple tasks on their own. You are helping to nurture strong, independent, and confident children, not leeches that cling to you constantly. That won't help them when they are off on their own in a class or in school. It's a question of understanding the perfect balance of when you should engage a child and be part of an activity and when the child is allowed to play independently.

Scenario:

Another nanny works with children whose parents are close friends with the family and kids you work with. The kids are about the same ages as the kids you work with—three and one-half and two and one-half years old. They often call for playdates, but you have one problem: every time they come over, the playdate is an absolute nightmare. There are fights, bites, broken toys, and frequent temper tantrums, but all the other nanny ever does is threaten to punish the kids with a timeout or an abrupt end of the playdate, but she never follows through.

The children constantly snack and are so out of control that, at the end of the playdate, all the kids are miserable, and her kids are on a sugar high. What's even more irritating is the nanny constantly excuses the way the kids act out, blaming their behavior on her employers' parenting style. How do you address this while protecting the kids' friendship and without hurting the nanny's feelings?

You deal with this situation with honesty and diplomacy. First, you need to address the situation with your employers, so they are aware of the problem. Then you need to speak with the other nanny to help come up with ways that may make the playdate experience more enjoyable for all. You can make a snack rule that will cut down on the kids' sugary snacks, which are undoubtedly culprits in the unpleasant behavior and meltdowns.

Whether it's the employers' parenting style or not, the kids need boundaries, and rules must be enforced at all times. Once those rules are broken, there should always be consequences, and they must be dealt with immediately. If all fails, it is then left up to your employers to decide whether to approach their friends about their kids' behavior in order to find a solution to the playdate nightmare.

ETHNIC CLINGING IN THE NANNY CIRCLE

People are generally more comfortable when they are paired with others who they can relate to, speak with in their indigenous languages, execute certain tasks the same way, eat the same foods, or share a value system. The same is true in the nanny circle. Take a look at your own people of influence, and look at nannies congregating at a playground. What you will find is that the Caribbean nannies are together; the Hispanic nannies are in a force; and the Asians, Europeans, and Africans all have their cliques based on their cultural similarities.

Although this may never change, the whole idea of "ethnic clinging" in the nanny world does not help you or the children in your care. It limits possibilities and interactions with kids outside your circle and also does not give you the opportunity as a nanny to step outside your comfort zone. Stepping outside your comfort zone allows you to be better rounded in various aspects of childcare, including conflict resolution, understanding childcare from a different culture's perspective, and, for non-English-speaking nannies, may help improve your language skills.

Children who are raised fully aware of other cultures and ethnic groups become young adults who find it easier to blend and adapt in an urban college where there's a lot of diversity. You can start that process by interacting with a whole melting pot of nannies from different ethnic groups and regions of the world. Set up a playdate with a nanny from a different background from you, with kids who are socially compatible, and get to know each other. You'll soon find out there are valuable things to learn. At the end, what makes us stronger as nannies, our undying love and respect for kids, is greater than what makes us different.

SNACKS, SNACKS, AND MORE SNACKS

We all need snacks during the day, and the same is true for toddlers and children. There are healthy fruit options, cheeses, yogurt, and vegetables that make great snacks and are rich sources of the vitamins and minerals developing kids need.

The problem with snacking is when it becomes excessive, includes only simple sugars or carbohydrates, and when snacks are used as rewards for fostering or increasing positive behaviors. For many nannies and sitters, giving snacks to a child is sometimes their way to quell tantrums and avoid dealing with a difficult childcare situation.

I've observed nannies handing a snack to a child who was engaged in some sort of unacceptable behavior as a way get the child to sit for a few minutes. This type of reward system is extremely dangerous, as it's a negative reinforcement, and it only promotes excessive snacking, which leads to what I term "Little Snack Monster" (LSMS) Syndrome. The little snack monsters can't go one hour without a snack and often have meltdowns if they don't get a snack. Many children with a high dependency on snacks suffer from bad eating habits. Because they are constantly full from eating snacks, they have problems eating their main meals.

Set designated snack times for children and ensure the snacks have nutritional value. Also increase the children's water intake, which may make them feel fuller and decrease their desire to snack.

WHAT'S THE IMPORTANCE OF DEVELOPING HEALTHY SLEEP PATTERNS IN YOUNG CHILDREN?

Just like food, water, and exercise, children need enough rest and sleep for proper mind and body development. With children having more scheduled school and after-school activities, parents working longer hours, and changes in family structure, more kids do not get the desired amount of sleep at night and also miss naps. Bedtimes are pushed later to accommodate meal preparation times or, when there's a nanny at home, to ensure that the parents spend time with their kids after a long day's work. As a result of kids also taking more enrichment classes, they get fewer naptimes, which may affect their temperaments as well as their social, cognitive, and learning abilities.

Children who don't nap are more likely to throw tantrums due to overexertion and overstimulation. Children who get adequate amounts of quality sleep are more alert and attentive and behave in a more socially acceptable manner.

In his book *Healthy Sleep Habits, Happy Child* Dr. Marc Weissbluth provides these insightful comments on the functions of sleep:

Sleep is the power source that keeps your mind alert and calm. Every night and at every nap, sleep recharges the brain's battery. Sleeping well increases brainpower just as weight lifting builds stronger muscles, because sleeping well increases your attention span and allows you to be physically relaxed and mentally alert at the same time. Then you are at your personal best.[1]

To help toddlers nap during the day, keep naptimes consistent. You can give a young child a soft toy, or give an older kid a comforting blanket. Also maintain consistency with your actions, including tucking the children in to sleep and telling them what they can look forward to upon awakening. Never go back and forth in the room if a child starts crying, as it will only exacerbate the problem.

Situation to avoid:

James is a two-year-old who was always a bad napper. His nanny understood he needed to nap, because he showed signs of tiredness and was inattentive. She insisted all James needed was the assurance that if he napped, he would feel better, and he could earn a reward. She knew if the mom cooperated, James would get the sleep he truly desired and would fall into a routine in a week or two.

Instead of embracing the nanny's suggestion, the mom, a petite-framed woman, often crawled into James's bed, and this was the only way he would nap. Sadly for this family, James got so used to his mom sleeping in his bed that he no longer slept in his room at night, creating a stressful situation for the family. They finally accepted the nanny's method of putting James to sleep which resulted in less stress and anxiety for all involved.

---

[1] Dr. Marc Weissbluth, *Healthy Sleep Habits, Happy Child* (New York: Random House INC, 1999)

WORKING WITH GAY AND LESBIAN COUPLES

Research now suggests more than 10 percent of same-sex couples are parenting a child, making them an important diverse group in society's family structure. A gay or lesbian couple's home is no different than the home of a heterosexual couple. Their value systems and their wishes for their kids to excel and be the best they can be are the same expectations and desires heterosexual parents have for their kids. The vast consensus shows that children growing up in same-sex parental households do not have differences in self-esteem, gender identity, or emotional problems from children growing up in heterosexual-parent homes.

As a nanny with the experience of working with gay parents, I know firsthand that those parents face unwarranted prejudices based solely on their sexual orientation and not on their skills as parents. Sadly, people often base those biased, preconceived notions on their own intolerances and a lack of knowledge, rather than on personal experiences or empirical evidence.

Since there are so many same-sex families raising children, it's safe to say there are many nannies working for those families. Nannies need to realize family dynamics, values, and structure are different in every home, regardless of whether it's the home of a heterosexual or same-sex couple. The parents' expectations of you as their nanny will be based on their own values and the parenting styles they use when raising their kids.

When working with kids with two dads, understand that you are not accepting the job to fulfill the role of mommy for the kids, nor are the parents wanting, or expecting, you to do that. Understand your boundaries as the employee and respect the family unit. Same-sex marriage is legal in many states in America and in many countries worldwide, so society is accepting the fact that same-sex families will have and raise children. It's no longer considered taboo. If people took the time to get to know others as individuals or as the parents they are, they would realize that same-sex parents have healthy family units just like other families do and are raising morally strong, respected kids in society. What makes them special is not the structure of their families, but who they are as individuals and the type of parents they are.

COMMON ENCOUNTERS A NANNY MAY FACE WHEN WORKING FOR SAME-SEX COUPLES

A nanny is in a supermarket with the twins she cares for, and a kind gentleman and his wife walk up to them and compliment the twins' appearance.

"They are so beautiful," the wife says, smiling to the kids.

"Your blue eyes are so striking," they continue with a pleasant smile on their faces. Of course they are just random strangers at the supermarket. But what they say next is a common comment.

The man leans over and kindly ask the kids, "Who has Mommy's looks and eyes, and which one of you looks like Daddy?"

Oops. It's the nanny's cue to butt in and save the day. "They look like Daddy," she replies and hurries to exit the supermarket.

The seemingly innocent couple might think the nanny was abrupt, but she was trying to avoid putting the three-year-olds in a situation that could have involved a lengthy explanation.

This scenario in itself taught me a lesson, which is to always try to be politically correct when dealing with kids. I make no references about their parents unless I know what type of family structure they have.

Also be on the alert for inquisitive parents who question you about the affairs of the same-sex family you work for. They are often just trying to comprehend the family dynamics, or they may simply be curious. I believe people often questioned me about the same-sex parents I worked for because they couldn't conceive there was as much structure and stability in their household.

Some of my best years as a nanny were while I worked for a gay couple for over seven years. Although the twins I cared for were the couple's first children, their paternal instincts kicked in right away and, before long, I was also learning from them. I saw the hope and love in their eyes for their children and that meant a lot to me as their caregiver. I respected them for who they were: loving parents who, in turn, respected and valued me as their caregiver.

It was during a time when society was not as open to same-sex families as it is now, and I often encountered negative people who knew nothing about the family dynamic but still made judgments about the family. I never entertained such behavior. Instead I rooted for those kind men, who were the best fathers I knew.

I was even more passionate about them because I was raised without my own father, and those children received double portions of love from their fathers. It dawned on me how hypocritical society is in that there's not that level of aggressiveness to call to task all the AWOL fathers who know nothing about their children, but we wanted to deny two loving men the opportunity to raise their own.

Today these kids are happy, well-adjusted children. I'll always love them, and they own a place in my heart. As for the gay couple, they taught me so much about love. They are like my own father, a father I never knew.

THE "THE NANNY MAFIA," A SERIOUSLY UNPRODUCTIVE CLAN. REFUSE ITS MEMBERSHIP.

Walk through any children's playground or outdoor park with children's amenities in a large city that has nannies, like New York, and guess what a common sight would be? "The Nanny Mafia," a group of nannies who usually sit on park benches near playgrounds, with expensive strollers containing babies and young children lined up.

These are the nannies who do not engage with the children at the park. Instead, they congregate to gossip, usually about their employers or other nannies outside their clans. With all this busy chatter going on, they distract the young children with snack cups when they could be enjoying the playground or slides.

Nanny Mafia members are usually boisterous, quick to offend others with their words, and, frankly, have double personalities—the good nanny image in the presence of the employers and the almost thuggish behavior outside. While these nannies never pose a threat to the safety of children, they only provide custodial care to them and refuse to go the extra mile. They are the non-engaging types, the phone addicts, the ones who have to be in the middle of a group of nannies and constantly debate everything but the well-being of the children they care for.

Attitudes of members of the Nanny Mafia are similar and are evident in their approaches and relationships with other nannies and parents. They are paranoid and believe every parent and nanny constantly monitors or evaluates their work to report it to their employers. Their paranoia manifests itself when they believe other nannies are looking for the opportunity to take their jobs. Obviously, the lack of confidence in their own job stability and the lack of trust in other people are the result of their poor efforts.

The Nanny Mafia would not be an appealing group to join for nannies who value their jobs. Deny their membership requests if they ever make them. Don't be naïve. The membership request is never formal but is an open invitation to gossip and to not engage in stimulating activities with the kids. There is nothing more valuable to a nanny than great, verifiable references and happy children from the past. These children are well aware of the positive impact you have made on their lives.

YOU ARE A LIVE-IN NANNY AND, LIKE EVERY WOMAN AND MAN, YOU HAVE SEXUAL NEEDS. WHAT IS A NANNY TO DO IN THIS SITUATION?

You live with a family for five, or even six, days a week, caring for their kids as their nanny. You may be married or have a significant other in your life, and you both have sexual desires you may be unable to fulfill because of your work commitments. This creates a level of frustration for both you and your partner and may negatively affect your emotions. What's a nanny to do when she just wants a little "something something?"

Some nannies work far from home, and commuting back and forth to work would be even more challenging, making a live-in job the better option. Likewise, there are situations where employers work far from home and their hours of work may fluctuate, like a doctor's. Under these circumstances, a live-in nanny may be the only option.

However, what I'll never understand is why a stay-at-home mom with one or two kids and a husband who is home at a decent hour every day needs a live-in nanny. Let's assume that while she does not work, her task load is significant, and hence the reason for a live-in nanny. Does she really need a nanny for five or six days a week, or is that perhaps her unwillingness to tend to her own kids? Her lack of consideration for the nanny's personal life, when the employer could spare the nanny time to visit her family but doesn't is troubling.

Perhaps she has never considered the nanny's inability to spend quality time with her own spouse or children. Has she ever reversed the roles and asked herself, "Could I do that?" Or does she completely disregard that aspect of the nanny's life and only see her as the caregiver?

Well, nannies, your personal needs should be as important to you as your job is, and no area of your life should be neglected or compromised. A balanced emotional life helps make you a better nanny and employee.

Before accepting any employment offer, especially one that requires you to be away from home, ensure that you understand the ramifications. Ensure both you and your spouse are in agreement with your working situation and find creative ways to spice up your intimate life with whatever time you have. Don't be naïve of the consequences of being an absent spouse week after week, month after month, or year after year.

Consider this:

Never allow your sexual desires to force you to into anything that might affect your relationship with your employers or your job stability. Irrational behavior, such as inviting your spouse to your employer's home, to fulfill your intimate needs without having the consent of your employer, is incomprehensible. Some nannies have lost their livelihoods because of their desires and spur-of-the-moment, irresponsible decision making. Not every shoe fits all feet, not every garment fits all bodies, and there are some situations that aren't for every nanny. Therefore, a lot of thought has to go into the decision to become a live-in nanny.

DON'T START WHAT YOU CAN'T FINISH. PEOPLE ARE CREATURES OF HABIT AND WILL PATTERN THEIR LIVES BASED ON YOUR PREDICTABLE SCHEDULE.

So you've secured this wonderful job caring for well-adjusted kids and absolutely love what you do...*great*! Your contract sets guidelines as it relates to your work schedule including hours, days, and time of work...*perfect*. You are scheduled to be at work at eight in the morning, but you see the need to be there at 7:15 every day. I commend you and applaud your efforts and due diligence.

However, there are several factors to consider before starting something you might not be able to finish. If you decide to start work this early, ensure it's a schedule you can be consistent with. Many nannies believe arriving at work early reflects how passionate they are about their jobs and ensures their jobs are secure, but this is just one aspect of job security.

In many instances, after the nannies become comfortable on the job, they abruptly begin arriving at work at the hours designated in their contracts, often without giving the employers any notice. I bet you're thinking "But that's the time I'm supposed to arrive at work." True, but the employers have likely scheduled their lives based on the generous forty-five minutes you volunteered to them in the first place.

Taking it away without notice creates frustration for the family. It's not surprising nannies often complain their employers seemed upset when they got to work at the designated time, instead of the thirty or forty-five minutes early they've spoiled them with.

I suggest before you start arriving at your employers' home forty-five minutes earlier, find out if it's OK with them. Some parents enjoy their alone time with their kids and use it as quality family time, whether they are cuddling in bed or bonding with the kids.

People with strong work ethics and values should be commended, but arriving at work forty-five minutes early to prove you are a quality employee robs you of valuable time that could be spent reading a self-improvement book, meditating, journaling, or simply enjoying some quality "me" time before the commencement of work.

Then, nanny, when it's time to report to work, ensure you're there *on time*.

NO ONE HAS THE RIGHT TO PHYSICALLY OR VERBALLY ABUSE YOU

I once heard a horrific story about an encounter a nanny had with her employer, who, during the early hours of the morning, suddenly appeared in her room in the family's pool house. She had been employed by that family for over two years. The family seemed normal, and she enjoyed all the perks and privileges of working for them in their beautiful beachfront property in the Hamptons they utilized on weekends in the summer months.

Astounded by his presence in her room, she grabbed the blanket to conceal her half-naked body. The intruder, her employer, walked close to her, leaned over, and told her how he wanted to express his appreciation for caring as well as she did for his children. Then he pressed his lips on hers and kissed her. The mortified and disgusted look on her face must have scared him, as he quickly retreated to the main house, where his wife slept.

That morning, he waited till his wife went out to play tennis with her friends, and then handed the nanny a check for more than four weeks' pay. Before he left the room, he reminded her he was a brilliant attorney with much influence in the Hamptons and in Manhattan. He threatened that if she told anyone what had happened earlier, he would ensure that she would never find employment in childcare. A high-class loser is my best description for this pervert.

If you live with a family, you should have a specific room designated to you, one with a door you can lock to ensure your own security. When you are in that room, if your employers need you, they should either call you on the phone or knock on the door and allow you time to dress appropriately before opening the door. No one has the right to suddenly enter your room without notice, as this violates your personal privacy.

I'm a strong proponent of webcams and believe every family with a nanny should have one in their home. However, the webcam installation must adhere to the guidelines set out by the state where the employer lives. In some cases, employers don't adhere to those guidelines and place webcams in bathrooms and in private rooms where the nanny lodges. "You damn peeping Toms." Placing a webcam in a bathroom also violates the employee's privacy, and employers may face stiff penalties by appropriate law enforcement agencies.

A few years ago, many news outlets carried the shocking news of a housekeeper being physically abused in Long Island, New York. People couldn't understand what prompted the perpetrators to behave in that appalling manner. Whatever the reason or situation, no one has the right to physically abuse you. You are protected under the same laws that protect others. Sexual advances and harassment should be promptly dealt with and reported to the necessary law authorities.

Verbal abuse by the employer is a common complaint among nannies, and this, too, must be swiftly dealt with to ensure it does not become habitual. Kids emulate their parents and caregivers, and every effort must be made to model appropriate behavior. Some employers see the need to strip nannies of their dignity and sense of self-worth by verbally abusing them in order to psychologically dominate them and ensure they remain submissive to them. This cowardly act is atrocious in itself.

When interviewing with a family, try to get insight into family values and moral construct and discuss yours candidly as well as your expectations and what you bring to the family in terms of morals and value system. Just as a family needs references from you before considering hiring you, get at least two references from the family, so you can make a more informed decision as to whether you want to work with them. Don't be intimidated to ask because the hiring parents would not accept a job from a company they know nothing about. They would be meticulous and vigilant in finding the information they need, and you, as the nanny, must do the same.

Lastly, you have to give respect to get respect. Ensure you present yourself respectfully in each situation; when it's not reciprocated, then it's your cue to move on.

EMERGENCY ACTION PLAN

Every family should have an emergency action plan in the event of an emergency that may affect the emotional and physical stability of the family, especially the children. What happens if both parents are at work and there's a terrorist attack in one of the big cities, and they're not able to return home?

The emergency action plan should have a series of actions and guidelines to guide the nanny during an emergency. It should include pertinent details, such as who the kids must be left with and telephone contacts for any member of the family you can entrust with the welfare and well-being of the kids, the pediatrician, and anyone who could be a support during an emergency. There should be open dialogue about what the nanny is allowed to do with the kids in the event of a crisis when both parents are away from home. All this important information must be written down and placed somewhere that is easily accessible.

A good emergency action plan should include a plan in the event of a terrorist attack; a plan for a natural disaster like an earthquake, fire, or storm; and a plan in case of sickness, accident, or even death. During and after Hurricane Sandy in the Northeast, many families evacuated their Manhattan apartments and homes, and countless nannies were unable to get to work or were stuck on their jobs. Some families opted to provide taxi services for the nannies to get to work, while others worked out a temporary live-in arrangement that was beneficial to both parties.

Then there were the employers who refused to pay their nannies, because they had no way to get to work.

Nannies, ensure you have an emergency action plan for your own family and children, especially in the event that you are stuck on the job due to an emergency. Designate a trusted friend or family member to oversee the safety of your kids in your absence, and perhaps the absence of your spouse as well. Ensure you understand the execution of those plans in the event of a real emergency.

Humorous corner:

Debbie, a nanny with almost ten years of service in the industry, was at work with the two kids she had cared for over the past three years. They were asleep, because it was their designated naptime, when Debbie felt the apartment shake. As she was on the ninth floor, she got a little alarmed but, for some reason, she thought a "bad spirit" had come into the apartment.

Debbie, an avid church attendee who could quote any scripture, grabbed the holy oil she carried with her everywhere. "Today you seem to be out for me," she shouted in her southern Caribbean accent. "But I rebuke you and cast you away." She anointed every door in the small apartment with the sign of the cross. Her act was indeed ironic, because Debbie worked with a Jewish family.

As she continued quoting every psalm she knew, her telephone rang, and the apartment shook once more. Realizing it was her employer, she dashed for the phone. Before she could say anything, her employer inquired whether she had felt the earthquake.

"Oh, you mean that was an earthquake?" Debbie said, embarrassed. At that point she closed her secret weapon, her holy oil, and placed it back in its sacred place in her bag.

When Debbie told me that story, I couldn't help but laugh until I cried, but there was a message in the laughter. As a caregiver, you should always be mindful of your environment and be a quick thinker who can make instantaneous and wise decisions at the spur of a moment.

DEALING WITH THE EXTENDED FAMILY WHILE CAREGIVING: THE GOOD, THE BAD, AND THE DREADED GRANDMA.

Year after year, month after month, week after week, you've cared for the same kids, respected the family's rules, and recognized the boundaries. However, the week the dreaded grandma comes to visit, everything seems to be in upheaval.

Fully understanding Grandma needs time to bond with her grandchildren—and rightfully so—you give her private time with the kids. However, nothing you do pleases Grandma: from the types of food you feed the kids, to the way you dress them, or even how you pronounce some words. How do you handle this situation with Grandma and ensure that the environment is pleasant to work in and relaxing for the kids?

First, if this grandma is bent on making you totally miserable while she visits and that you do things the way she suggests, it will be difficult to handle the situation without discussing it with your employers. Your employers then need to address the matter immediately with the grandmother and find out what her concerns are as they relate to your care of her grandkids. She must be told that while her ideas and advice are invaluable and that the family welcomes her feedback, they have their own set of rules, value system, and manner of doing things, which are the guidelines you, the nanny, follow. The employers must ensure the feedback from the grandparents about your performance is based on credible, truthful, non-biased judgment. Any concerns must be brought up to you in the presence of the hiring family.

As much as possible, continue to show the grandmother respect, and be mindful that the time she spends with her grandchildren may be invaluable bonding time, especially if she does not live in the same city as they do. Invite her to help in the day-to-day care of the kids, including feeding, bathing, and changing them. Take a backseat in the care of the kids, and follow the grandparents' lead as long as the safety of the kids is not compromised, especially in the case of aging grandparents.

If Grandma is still unhappy, and you've tried your best, it is now her problem to deal with as long as it does not cause you sleepless nights. Sadly, there are a few grandmas like this.

TAKE TIME OFF FOR YOURSELF

Monday is usually the busiest day of the week for nannies. One particular Monday in early spring seemed like the *longest* day, because I was overwhelmed with the news of yet another nanny dying over that weekend. As I approached a busy kids' playground at Madison Avenue, I vividly remember seeing the pockets of nannies who had congregated. The seriousness on their faces told me that something tragic had happened. It's easy to get filled in on the information at any park, especially if the news is grave. Any of the nannies will be eager to tell you who got fired, how big a bonus another nanny received, and who is moving to a new city. You can go through the bowels of someone's life in a minute with a nanny who is a chatter or who loves to gossip.

That morning it was the news of the untimely death of a thirty-two-year-old nanny, a native from Jamaica who had only been at the playground two weeks prior, laughing with other nannies in their circle of friends. She seemed healthy and full of life, so the news weighed heavily on our minds and hearts.

One conversation that resonated among nannies that day was the need for them to care for themselves, just as they care for others. Most nannies work long hours and miss doctor's appointments and yearly checkups and would rather numb a physical pain, because they do not have the luxury or good fortune of taking a personal day off to visit the doctor. Even when they have a doctor's appointment, some employers call them often to see if they are through with their doctor's visit.

A jovial nanny once shared the story of having a pap smear done while receiving a barrage of texts from her employer, who was inquiring about what time the nanny would get to work to relieve her so she could go to the gym. Ironic indeed! A woman who is so concerned about her health and body image and would never miss a gym appointment frustrates another while she is getting a test that could mean life or death.

Because most nannies never get medical or health benefits, they neglect a lot of important health issues. This neglect results in the deterioration of known medical ailments by the nanny.

Yes, nannies...yes, you! The one who could barely stand straight when you bend over to pick a young child up. It's time to seriously think about your health and request the necessary time off to visit the doctor. A job will always be around, but some health issues require immediate attention. For the thousands without medical benefits, be aware there are health clinics in most towns that supply superior services, and most tests can be done right at those facilities. Good health is more valuable than cash, and it is what will allow you to earn a living.

HOW DO YOU DEAL WITH THE MOM WITH THE "ACCESSORY BABIES"?

You work with a family with a stay-at-home mom, yet you feel like all the weight of caring for her child is on you. Mom is constantly busy while you are on a twelve-hour shift; she's either entertaining girlfriends, shopping, or spending every hour at yoga, pilates, or gym classes and never gives you, the caregiver, a break during the day.

Forget about a break for you for a minute, and think about whether she has enough time to bond with her own children, which is important for healthy emotional and psychological development. Since you spend a lot of time with the children, there is a clear emotional bond between you, and you can see that Mom is visibly upset when the kids cry after you.

This hypocrisy is evident in many homes. The number of parents who neglect to be part of the overall care of their own children is shocking. Some parents think the nanny has to work as long as it's the designated time to work, and while this statement is accurate, I beg the question: Why can't a stay-at-home mom spend a half hour with a young child putting puzzle pieces together, visiting a neighborhood park, or playing dress-up? What's more frustrating about this trend is this same mom, who is usually MIA in the care of her kids, suddenly becomes "supermom" if she has an audience. If the in-laws are visiting, or if she is in the company of mothers with kids in a similar age group, you may be shocked to see Mom turn into an actress.

This is why some nannies call these kids "accessory babies." It's like putting on a piece of jewelry to complement a beautiful dress. There is a way to handle her and ensure the kids you care for are psychologically, emotionally, and physically stimulated.

Once you have identified what this mother's parenting style is, it's your choice to either work with it or opt out. If you decide you can deal with it, for goodness' sake, stop complaining. It is what it is… handle it. Erase your high expectations of this parent as it relates to assistance with the care of the child. Do your best while you work your shift to ensure a healthy balance for that child. If you notice signs that the absence of Mom bothers or affects the child negatively, address it with the parent.

You are a paid employee, and you cannot control what your employer does with her time and where she places her child within her value system. Just ensure you are giving the deserving child the best possible care.

NEW ADDITION TO THE FAMILY

Good news! Your employer is having another baby, and there is so much to be excited about. The new addition to the family often affords you the job stability you need, because the older kids are getting ready to start school.

What's your new role in the baby's life, and have your employers made necessary adjustments in your compensation, vacation time, and hours of work? If these questions are not addressed by your employer, which is often the case, the burden is on you to ensure you are paid fairly, your new job description is fully outlined, and you are comfortable and capable of caring for the new baby.

There is no set norm as it relates to the new addition to a family and the role for an existing nanny. Everything depends on several factors, such as a family's financial situation, their generosity toward the existing nanny, the work demands, and the employee skill set. While some families seek an additional pair of hands to take care of the new baby, others work out a comfortable package with their current nanny that is mutually rewarding.

I advise nannies to take some vacation time prior to the arrival of the new baby in order to be rejuvenated and ready for the physical demands of caring for, in some situations, both young children and newborns at the same time.

What about the families who make no provisions or who expect that everything, as it relates to the care of their kids, will be left the same even with an additional child to care for? This is preposterous and disrespectful to the nanny. When a family factors the cost of having another child, they must be mindful of additional childcare expenses and be fully prepared to absorb that cost if they require a nanny. It's not a free-for-all when it comes to the services and care rendered by a qualified nanny. Don't take it for granted that, since she was hired to care for your kids, the number of kids does not matter.

Consider your own work life if you are an employee. Imagine management gives you additional job responsibilities or more hours of work without a pay increase. I heard you! "They must be kidding me, right?" you would've muttered. That's what the nanny thinks when you don't make provisions for the additional job responsibilities you are asking her to assume. Even when some employees will hold on to this work situation, they will not be happy.

Parents, you never want someone who is unhappy with their work situation anywhere close to your children. While the nanny may not physically harm the kids, she may not go the extra mile for you or them.

Communication and respect are two powerful ingredients in a successful nanny-family relationship. Therefore, show you have some regard for the person who takes care of the most important people in your life and compensate duly. A happy nanny goes the extra mile for the kids she cares for. Please never forget that, parents.

I AM NOT YOUR SUPERWOMAN…I GET TIRED TOO

Caring for children is not only a rewarding task but can also be a daunting one, keeping up with the demands and schedules of children. Ask any stay-at-home mom or nanny. Most nannies work, on average, between ten and thirteen hours daily and care for an average of two kids. Their daily activities include the custodial care of the kids, such as feeding, bathing, and changing soiled diapers, and the enrichment aspects of caregiving, like reading to the kids, coloring, and painting. We need to also factor in the enrichment outside the home the kids attend, on average three times per week, like ballet, gymnastics, dancing, and cooking. All the activities are coordinated by the nanny and can be physically demanding. We have not taken into consideration the nights this nanny may have to work overtime, so the employers can have some spousal time or attend business functions.

This is indeed quite a job and will leave the best of nannies tired. So why is it that some employers see the need to have their nannies work every Saturday, giving them only one day off per week under those conditions? The one day a week off the employer ironically instructs you to find time to rest.

This is an increasing trend that involves the utmost disregard of the nanny. It is as though the parents think the nanny does not get tired. In fact, most of these employers see their nannies as superwomen whose lives are centered around them.

If the nanny is a mother or a wife, how can she juggle her own family when she gives all her time to her employer? Nannies who tolerate these working conditions are often women with few choices, such as the ones whose employers sponsor them in the United States, and they feel like they owe them their lives. Those employers may not have considered the nanny's young kids are just as valuable as theirs and have the same emotional and physical needs.

Hello nannies, understand there are many wonderful and understanding families that are eager to welcome a professional and caring nanny to complement their family. If you are not happy with your job situations, it will consequently affect your performance and even the relationship with the kids you care for.

You should not work for anyone who disrespects you, your services, your family, and especially your kids. The economic stability they provide does not mean the world should revolve around them, or you should completely neglect your own life to make them happy. A successful nanny-employer relationship starts with mutual trust, respect, and consideration for each other.

DISHONESTY

There is no place for dishonesty while caring for kids. Your employer's personal items will always be their personal items. Her jewelry box and its contents have nothing to do with you. Certainly items removed from the residence without the consent of your employer would be considered stealing. Stealing carries severe penalties, including jail time in all US states.

DON'T ALLOW THE IGNORANT ACTS OR ATTITUDES OF EMPLOYEES OR MANAGEMENT OF THE RESIDENTIAL BUILDING WHERE YOU WORK DEFINE YOU AS A NANNY

The majority of nannies who work in large metropolitan cities work in private residential buildings, most of which have doormen, building management personnel, and other staff. Hence the nannies indirectly build a working and social relationship with the building staff.

The disregard for the value of a nanny that exists in some buildings is shocking. In some situations, nannies are forbidden to use the basic amenities of the building, such as the health club, because they are not considered a part of the family that resides in the building. For the nannies who live with the family for sometimes six days a week, this exclusion is outright repulsive. The hypocrisy is the same building personnel allow the families' guests, who also do not reside in the buildings, to enjoy the amenities without a problem. This is definitely not the standard and varies from one building to another.

Some doormen will not open the door for a nanny but open it for every resident or visitor. The lack of courtesy and regard given to nannies by these individuals reflects their negative opinions about the nanny profession. While the attitudes and lack of professionalism of some nannies helps feed that repulsive behavior, there are still many people out there who need to understand and respect the value a good nanny brings to a family.

These nannies are not able to sit in the waiting area to enjoy a cup of coffee or read a newspaper. This ignorance reminds me of the days when domestic workers were not allowed to use the same restrooms as their employers. While nannies cannot prevent anyone from believing the stereotypes, they can certainly help foster a greater respect for themselves by conducting themselves in a professional manner at all times.

Nannies should always keep a professional relationship with the building staff and avoid gossip and cheap rhetoric about their employers' affairs. Respect and adhere to the rules of the building where you work and demand the respect you deserve.

There are also great staff and management at some buildings who are accommodating to nannies and treat them with dignity and respect. I applaud and respect that approach, which is certainly not the norm.

So, nannies, it doesn't matter where you work, whether it's in a private residence or a public building, the negative opinions of others are inconsequential. What truly matters is that you and your attitude do not encourage negative stereotypes and uninformed beliefs about such a wonderful profession.

A NANNY IS A NANNY—NOT A COOK, HOUSE MANAGER, REFRIGERATOR CLEANER, CLOTHES IRONER, DOG WALKER, OR WINDOW WASHER

It is extremely difficult to juggle a crying or fussy infant and clean a home. One of the major complaints of nannies is the lack of understanding by employers that these two tasks cannot be executed with the quality they expect. A nanny who is hired to ensure the safety and well-being of a child has no time or business cleaning your home, ironing your clothes, sorting your trash, shopping in the supermarket, or running every errand on your personal to-do list.

While a great nanny is also a great multitasker who may take on tasks around the house to help the household function better, the problem is the expectation of some of the employers. Yes, I'm talking about the ones with three kids, two dogs, and a cat who expect that the children's clothes are ironed, the refrigerator is cleaned, dinner is prepared every night, the kids are taken to classes blocks away from home, and the kids are bathed and in their pajamas, so that within a half hour of the parents getting home from work, the kids are ready for bed. Are you for real, Mom and Dad?

What's also frustrating is the double standard, because those same parents are not embarrassed to tell the nannies and others when the weekend comes, everything is in upheaval around the house and they can't wait for the nanny to come back on Monday mornings. The reason for the organizational chaos is their own inability to juggle the kids and care for the home, so why are the expectations on the nanny greater? I know that Mary Poppins gives us the illusion she can fly, but nannies don't have magical wands that makes things happen. It takes effort, hard work, commitment, and a lot of stress to function in this capacity.

A job that should really be designated to two people but is done by one and sacrifices the proper care of the kids is idiotic. Parents, who are guilty of this, please take a second and figure it out—that's all the time you'll need. Many of the guilty employers are suburban employers who did not factor in the cost of housekeeping and childcare they would incur when they moved to the suburbs. The next best option is the nanny who'd care for the kids and also handle all the housekeeping tasks.

Another troubling aspect of this problem is most of the nannies doing these demanding jobs are paid minimum wages. Sad, but these are the hidden secrets in this industry everyone pretends not to be aware of. This is America, right?

There are situations where a nanny's job can be combined with housekeeping duties, and everyone involved is happy, such as when a family has school-aged children, and the nanny willingly agrees to include some housekeeping duties. Other scenarios, such as when there is a contributing stay-at-home parent who helps with the children while the nanny performs household chores, are fair if both parties agree, and everyone pulls their weight.

A Guide to Developing a Successful Family ...

Every situation is different, so be aware of what you agree to as a job description, and ensure it's realistic. Be mindful that caring for children is one of the hardest jobs there is and, when making a decision about a particular job, ensure you are fully capable of executing the job functions without compromising your physical, mental, and emotional well-being.

No nanny can be a cook, housekeeper, house manager, playmate, tooshie wiper, fight separator, and enrichment-class juggler all at the same time. One or many things will not receive the amount of time and effort needed. As a nanny, ensure it's not the happiness and well-being of the kids that is compromised. If you happen to be a nanny with an insurmountable, non-practical to-do list, it's time to tear, burn, or flush that list, and find a family with more realistic expectations.

HELLO, MANNIES!

That is not a typo. I meant to write mannies. All those wonderful male caregivers who are just as skilled as their female counterparts in executing the perfect care plans for kids but who few people know about. Many "mannies" have successfully integrated into families and help provide both custodial and enrichment care for the kids they work with.

When parents are looking for a nanny to care for their children, many automatically interview only female nannies. The general perception is female nannies make better caregivers, hence male nannies put in double the effort to prove their abilities, skills, and trustworthiness because of their gender.

There are several factors to consider if a family contemplates a male nanny. Pros include the fact that male nannies usually love the outdoors and use an active, sports-oriented approach in their childcare services. They are more apt to be adventurous and spend fun times in sports-oriented activities. For single mothers, a good male nanny gives the children a positive male influence in their day-to-day activities.

Although single moms raise children effectively, children need a balance in their lives in terms of gender differences, and a male nanny can enable that. A male nanny could also complement a family with young, active boys and for parents with a single child who is a boy, simply because children respond better to same-sex adults, and boys may take instructions and guidance from a male nanny with fewer complaints.

Hiring a male nanny may not be easy, because a family's options are limited, as few males pursue a career in childcare, making finding the best complement for your family harder.

For the vast majority of families, the primary goal is the safety and overall happiness of the children and finding someone who provides a high caliber of care and is compatible with the family and their values and lifestyles.

With the face of American families changing daily, and the fact that more states are approving same-sex marriages, we will undoubtedly see an increasing need for conventional childcare to change as well. Society needs to erase the stereotypes of male caregivers and not draw uneducated conclusions about the level and quality of childcare they can provide. Consider the number of single dads raising their children, whether they are boys or girls, with a high level of competence. The same is true about men who decide that their true passion is caring for children and who ultimately become male nannies.

The first rule in choosing someone, male or female, to care for your kids is to consider the needs of your children and their individual personalities. Some kids are introverts and may be better suited with a soft-spoken, female nanny, whereas some little girls may be outgoing and may look to kick a few soccer balls outside with a male nanny.

Whatever you decide, conduct an extensive background check, whether it's a male or female nanny. Allow this individual to spend some time with your children, and observe the interactions with your kids carefully. My golden rule is to invest in a nanny cam, so you know exactly what's happening with your kids.

As it relates to hiring a caregiver, there are no set rules that fit all. In the end, your children's safety, happiness, and overall well-being take precedence over the norm.

To all the brilliant male nannies who love the childcare profession, keep doing a wonderful job making children's lives better.

HOW DO YOU WORK FOR A FAMILY THAT HAS A TOTALLY DIFFERENT VALUE SYSTEM THAN YOUR OWN?

One of the keys to being able to work in such an intimate setting as a family's home is to accept and respect the family's rules, value system, ideology, and beliefs. If their values are so far from yours that they cause conflict with the family, then you must look for a more compatible family to work for.

Another important consideration is that the family's parenting style is, to some extent, consistent with yours in order to send a clear message to the children about rules, boundaries, rewards, and consequences for breaking the rules.

There are, however, parents who will parent a certain way that maybe outright inappropriate, and you, as the caregiver, must allow your sound judgment and common sense to prevail.

Case in point:

Thomas, a three-year-old boy, cries every morning and refuses to eat breakfast. His mom says if he were hungry, he would definitely eat and gives him a small pack of candies to calm him down. He immediately calms down, and you the caregiver watch in amazement.

Because you have open dialogue with the parents, you tell the mom you believe her approach is not correct, but she fails to see that. As she always reminds you, she's an educated woman. The subliminal message she sends is you may not have a formal education, and this prevents you from assessing such a clear situation.

The mom doesn't realize the child associates crying with getting candies, and he cries to get what he wants. No one needs a formal education to decipher this. It's plain common sense. The mother is unconsciously encouraging an undesired behavior by constantly giving the child candies when he cries and hence he cries to get the candies.

In this situation the nanny should not be forced to adopt the same parenting model used by the mother which is frankly counterproductive. There are ways the nanny can get the child to eat and may reward him after breakfast if the mom insists he has candies. The nanny can remind him of the playdate she has set up with his friend later in the morning or the trip to the park or play space and explain to him he must eat in order to enjoy the things she has planned for him. The average three-year-old will soon start a conversation about something the nanny mentioned, and once the child's thought pattern changes, it's more than likely the child will eat. Whatever you have promised the child as a reward must be executed in order to develop trust.

Nannies must be mindful families' value systems differ considerably, and they must be careful not to compare one family to another or a past employer to the present one. The overall factor is ensuring the safety, well-being, and emotional stability of the child is not comprised by any individual and, yes, this includes some parents.

A Guide to Developing a Successful Family ...

You must not impose your own value system and religious beliefs on a child you care for if they contradict those of the family. If you work in an Orthodox Jewish, Muslim, or Sikh home, understand and educate yourself about their beliefs before you find yourself in an awkward position. Wait till you get home to have your pork chops if you are working at the Abduls', who are Muslims, or save your curry beef for the weekend if you work in the home of Indian Sikhs who are strict vegans.

THE GENEROSITY OF A FAMILY CANNOT ALWAYS BE MEASURED IN DOLLARS AND CENTS

Working in someone's home as a nanny allows you to build a close, familial relationship with the children and the parents. This close relationship often develops over a period of time when the family is fully able to trust you. In this type of setting, many families open their homes and even their resources to their caregivers and, in many cases, help make their lives better.

In rewarding nanny-family relationships, some families become extremely generous to the caregivers, who enjoy perks for their efforts and hard work. It's not uncommon to hear nannies boast of receiving monetary gifts, shopping sprees, bonuses, vacations, and even spa treatments. There are kind employers out there who treat their nannies with dignity and respect and who do exceedingly generous things for them.

Are these perks the only measure of an employer's generosity? *No!* There are also wonderful, generous employers who show their gratitude with measurable things like time off for the nanny to meet a personal deadline or to spend quality time with their own children on school breaks, and some are generous with immeasurable things like providing guidelines, guidance, and counsel for nannies who may experience personal conflicts and so forth.

Therefore, nannies, evaluate your own set of circumstances and appreciate the things a family does for you apart from the dollars and cents they pay. Do not compare what one family does for their employee with what yours may do for you. That's not the only measure of someone's gratitude. Remember that families' financial situations are all different, and people's generosity differs. The only thing the employers *must* give you is payment for your services, and they are in no way obliged to do anything extra, whether it's monetary or non-monetary.

For those who have the good fortune of working for generous employers, please reciprocate. Remember their anniversary, birthdays, and some holidays and give your time freely for them to have a private dinner. Remember the children's birthdays and milestones, and celebrate those also. Do not be only on the receiving end of generosity. It's in poor taste, no matter how much resources the family has.

Families, do not hold your employees hostage because of your generosity by reminding them of all you do whenever you want something extra, like their time. The beauty of giving is not in expecting anything in return but in letting it flow from the kindness of a good heart.

PERKS ON THE JOB

If a family can comfortably offer a caregiver benefits, they should. While realizing that families do have budgets, they can make benefits cost effective. If you offer a nanny a competitive package, that caregiver is more likely to make a long-term commitment. A family can offer benefits like holiday pay, sick and vacation pay, and, in some cases, health insurance, which is an attractive incentive. This ultimately makes the caregiver feel like a true professional and may result in greater productivity on the job.

Treat the caregiver with respect by understanding the need for time off and make provisions for personal days based on the individual state's guidelines. Any employee who is overworked, and does not find that healthy balance between work and personal life, will be resentful of the employer.

REGULARLY EXPRESS APPRECIATION. SAY THANK YOU.

Research shows that the ratio of positive to negative interactions is five to one in a successful relationship. You need not pay a caregiver five compliments before offering criticism, but parents must be mindful of the ratio, and understand everyone loves their efforts to be acknowledged.

People often neglect to say thank you especially when a service is being paid for. But a simple thank you makes people feel appreciated. Parents should take time to thank the caregiver for being a pillar of strength when a child is having a behavioral issue. They should say thank you for invaluable input that helped dissipate a tense situation. Indirectly the children will learn the importance of thanking someone who adds value to their lives. A good caregiver who feels appreciated by employers is more likely to display exceptional performance.

Caregivers should thank the parents for choosing them to share invaluable memories with their children. They should thank parents for the gift card they graciously gave for a birthday. They should let them know they appreciate and respect the parents. These simple acts will help nurture a strong relationship within the home.

IF A FAMILY HAS HAD THREE OR FOUR NANNIES IN ONE YEAR, RUN. SOMETHING IS WRONG!

Run, nanny, run! If you are interviewing with a family and find out that they've used the services of four or more nannies in a given year, it's your cue to run. There is something wrong with this picture. I'm not referring to the services of occasional babysitters who may come on weeknights or weekends to care for the kids.

One of the first signs of a troubled family is one who's not able to retain the services of a nanny long-term. It's unlikely all three or four nannies had a problem, and the actual problem likely lies with the family. Are the parent's expectations greater than the norm, are they difficult to work for, or are they simply hard to please?

While running a small nanny agency in New Jersey many years ago, I came across a mom who had gone through at least four nannies in a two-month period. I listened attentively as she blurted out her complaints with the nannies she'd employed. She complained about the scent of one's perfume; that her two-month old baby did not smile when she saw another, which to her signaled that something was wrong with the nanny; and every nonsensical thing one could imagine. To top it off, she boasted she was offering a top-notch job with high pay, which was $500 for an almost sixty-hour week. Clearly this woman had a big problem, and the only thing sadder is there are lots of people like her.

Families, it is important for children to have as much consistency and stability in their care arrangements as possible. Changing nannies often infringes on the emotional security of your children and is a dangerous practice. Consider how a child feels getting to know so many different people in a short space of time and trying to get acclimated to new temperaments, attitudes, and faces. In the best of all worlds, most parents want a good nanny who will stay until their child goes off to college! Unfortunately, all parents know even the best-planned childcare arrangements are fragile, and transitions from one caregiver to another are inevitable, but they must make every effort to ensure there is a consistent childcare regimen.

Nannies, when you meet employers who have unrealistic expectations or have used the services of countless nannies, heed this as a warning and run. There's always a better opportunity down the block.

A NANNY IS MOVING ON. HOW CAN THE PARENTS AND THE NANNY MAKE IT EASIER FOR THE CHILDREN TO COPE?

One of the saddest aspects of this profession is eventually the nanny has to move on, either because the child is grown and is in school full-time or grown enough to be in college. This is the wish of most parents. There are also situations where economics, medical emergencies, or families relocate to different areas or states leave the nanny little choice but to move on.

Many people believe the transition is easy. The thought process is that the kids will soon have a replacement nanny, the nanny will find another suitable family, and all will be well, but this is not as easy as it may sound. When working with children, close emotional connections develop. Kids gravitate to anyone who shows them affection, especially their nannies, who generally spend a considerable amount of time with them and are engaged in every aspect of their lives. For the nanny, the attachment is just the same. The kids become an integral part of her life, and it is impossible to not genuinely love them. When the time comes to move on, in order for everyone involved to continue to be emotionally healthy, they must take caution.

Young children must be given enough notice their nanny is moving on and reassurances they will have access to her by telephone, mail, and visits. They need to understand they did not cause the nanny to leave, and they will always be an important part of the nanny's life. If the nanny is moving on to a different family, she should avoid talking about those children with the current children, as they may feel rejected by her.

If at all possible, ease the transition by gradually decreasing the nanny's hours, so the children will get used to her not being around. The parents should have open conversations with the children about their feelings concerning the nanny moving on and encourage them to talk about it or even draw pictures that can give insights into their true feelings. Allow the children to freely express their emotions, and remind them it is perfectly fine to feel sad, angry, frustration, and even fearful, because the nanny is moving on. Explain to the children why the change is necessary, and ease their anxiety by reminding them of the love and support the parents provide.

Try to make the nanny the only change taking place. Situations where there is a divorce, a change of school or home as well as a change of nanny all at once, creates more frustration for children, exacerbates an already stressful situation and makes it more difficult for them to cope.

Parents may also be anxious and worried about the impending change, but they must exhibit positive and upbeat emotions, as their children will model their behavior. Likewise, even though it may be just as sad for the nanny, she must not exhibit raw emotions like anxiety and crying, because that will make the children sad and anxious too.

A change in caregiver is undeniably a tough situation for all parties involved. The good news is children are resilient and will adapt well, if given enough time to prepare and if they have the support of their parents. They are great at making emotional adjustments when the situation is effectively handled by all the caring parties in their lives. It's a time when care, love, and support within the family must take precedence for the healthy emotional well-being of all involved, particularly the children.

●

FINDING BALANCE AND TRANQUILITY IN A JOB THAT COULD BE STRESSFUL, EMOTIONALLY AND PHYSICALLY

I can't overstate the rewards of working with children and enjoying their milestones and physical and cognitive development. For many, caring for children from birth up to adolescence is a great accomplishment. However, caring for children can also be stressful. The workdays are long and the children's activities, such as enrichment classes, treks to the park, doctor appointments, playdates, birthday parties, and school can also be physically demanding. How does a nanny achieve balance to avoid getting burned out? How does she reserve enough energy to effectively care for her own kids after a long day of work?

It's important to develop a schedule for children, including a scheduled time to nap, eat, play, or have downtime. Routine encourages and establishes good habits and behavior and gives older children a sense of stability and the awareness about what needs to be done. Schedules and routines are also important, because children like to know what happens next. This reduces their anxiety and gives them a sense of security.

For example, children on a schedule know after the playground, they can expect lunch, and then naptime. If this schedule is consistent, children will learn the pattern, and most of the tasks that may cause temper tantrums or meltdowns, like naptimes, will be easier. This also allows caregivers to set aside some downtime for themselves to avoid the pitfall of being overly tired and burned out.

Parents should continue the weekday schedules and routines on the weekends. When schedules are unpredictable on the weekends and in the evenings, children exhibit inappropriate behavior. While it may be difficult to keep the schedule, especially on weekends, which may be the only time working parents have to run errands or personal appointments, I highly recommend keeping two important routines: meals and naps. If these two times are kept on schedule, the children's anxiety levels will drop; they will not be tired or hungry, thus reducing meltdowns.

When a scheduled time can't be met, such as a delay at lunchtime due to a doctor's appointment, always have a backup plan such as a healthy snack, in order to diffuse the situation when the child is upset or even crying. Effective scheduling and established routines can ease a lot of stress for caregivers.

Being able to multitask will not decrease the workload of a caregiver, but it will allow you to execute basic functions faster and give you some time when you can slow down to eat or mediate. It's incredible how reenergized you can feel after a quiet forty minutes while the kids nap. Just like children, adults who are tired are also fuzzy and more prone to making mistakes.

Exercise increases energy and gives you an overall feeling of well-being. All caregivers must ensure exercise is part of their lifestyle. Since many work long hours, they must be creative and innovative about exercising. While I was caring for newborn twins, I walked along the Hudson River early in the mornings with the babies lying comfortably in their stroller. They enjoyed the cool breeze from the Hudson, and the motion of the stroller soothed them to sleep. Their parents loved that the twins were outdoors in the morning before the blazing heat of the midday sun in the summer. Everyone was happy, and I got the exercise I needed, which gave me enough energy to care for those little bundles.

Being outdoors at a park or near a river or lake provides an atmosphere of tranquility and calmness, and if your work situation involves caring for newborns or infants, this could be a good time to read a self-help or motivational book while the children nap. Not only would it help you see things in a different way, it might also offer insights into many personal questions you may have. Reading motivational material also makes you feel good emotionally. I recommend Dr. Wayne Dyer, who is a great motivational speaker, and Dr. Phil, who always gives sound advice about parenting and other challenging and important life aspects.

THE DREADED MONDAY

You've said good-bye on a Friday and headed home to your own house after a long week at work. It certainly has not been easy, because the kids have mastered throwing tantrums, the classes you attend with the kids are becoming more now, and the workload is greater. This situation can be magnified for nannies who care for multiple children, sometimes of different ages. By the end of the week, however, everything seemed to fall into place: the kids have settled better, the home was organized, and things were running smoothly.

What on earth happens on the weekend? This is one of the most frequent questions nannies have at the beginning of the week. They can't understand why the house is in disarray with toys all over the floor, with dishes from the weekend's food preparation stacked on the stove, and with the laundry basket over pouring; the house looks like a tornado just ran through it. What's frustrating for those nannies is they keep things organized independently five days a week, but on the weekends, when both parents are available in some situations at the home, things are as crazy as they are.

My personal opinion is a lot of those parents believe there is someone who will pick up after them, so not much thought is placed on ensuring things are the way they should be. This shows a lack of regard for the caregiver, as she now has to juggle childcare duties with maintaining the home.

These parents must realize these are two different job functions, and it's not the job of the caregiver to pick up after them or organize their homes. Why can't a parent throw in a load of laundry or prepare dinner for their kids once a week? Why can't one parent do the weekly grocery shopping? Why can't some parents bathe their kids or shampoo their hair on the weekends? Why can't reasonable parents who are not disorganized teach their own kids to clean up after themselves? Simple things like cleaning up a playroom, which involves picking up toys off the floor, or preventing the kids from throwing every bit of clothes from their drawer, can be executed by a good parent. This should not be the job of the caregiver to sort through on Monday.

You may think I am exaggerating, but no, this is the Monday reality for a lot of caregivers in this country. The level of disorganization in some of these homes is shocking and outright disrespectful to the people who have to pick up the pieces and bring some sort of normalcy to the home.

On Mondays, a lot of caregivers are also faced with children who are extra whiny and quick to throw tantrums when things are not given to them or when they can't get their own way. The consensus among nannies is some parents overcompensate on the weekends, and the kids are rewarded, even when their behavior does not warrant it, in an effort to avoid a tantrum the parents have to deal with. So, for example, if the kids want candies before breakfast, then candies it is. If they want to sit in front of the television for hours, then television it is.

Who, then, are the adults in these relationships? Parents must take the lead and understand children need their guidance in doing the right thing. Shockingly though, those same parents will tell their

A Guide to Developing a Successful Family ...

nannies to ensure that appropriate rules are followed, such as no candies before breakfast and limits on watching television or playing video games, and then break those rules to make parenting easier for them. The lack of consistency is noticed even by young children, who will not hesitate to tell a caregiver whatever she's trying to make them do is not approved by their parents. Lack of consistency in parenting and childcare creates kids who defy rules, throw tantrums, and have no respect for authority, including their caregiver. Parents should also not forget to correct inappropriate behavior.

Parents must remember they are not raising children who will be confined to their private residences, but strong boys and girls, men and women of tomorrow, who must understand the world does not revolve around them, rules have to be adhered to and authority respected, and things will not always be done their way. That's where well-rounded people come from, from homes with parents who understand and appreciate a good value system for their children. At the end of the day, family economics, status quo, and influence do not matter if their children become difficult to deal with at school, activities, or play.

I believe in the theory of innate goodness, that every child was born good. But we, as parents, must ensure we set our children with a good foundation, rules and values, to foster that innate goodness.

If you are one of those parents who forgets to perform some of the basic parenting obligations on the weekend with the great expectation that on Monday, the nanny will arrive to do what you should have done, bookmark this page. Straighten up around the house a little, encourage your kids to pick up the toys off the floor, stack the dishes in the dishwasher, and then you can continue reading this book.

When I worked as a nanny, the family became like my own family. I was protective of their privacy and never violated the respect they rightfully deserved. Whatever I saw in their home remained in their home. Nannies', talking about personal detail of a particular family is unprofessional, rude, and disrespectful. They need the same respect you deserve. Besides, when you look at the children you care for and love, you see the need to protect their parents because of how much you love the kids.

Happy Monday, parents and caregivers!

WHAT DO YOU DO AS THE CAREGIVER WHEN THE CHILD CALLS YOU MOMMY?

You may be the caregiver, the babysitter, the friend, but you are certainly not Mommy! It is natural and common for kids to call their caregivers Mommy at one point or another. But what's not natural is for the nanny to answer to that name, which encourages the behavior. Of course a nanny who loves a child feels good knowing the child loves her back, but a good caregiver will help the children understand her role in their lives.

Usually children call nannies Mommy to get their attention or to ask for something. If you constantly meet the child's needs after being called Mommy, you unconsciously enforce the behavior. Before filling the need, remind the child of your name and reference the mom in the conversation. Tell the child Mommy is at work or out and can't wait to hug the child when she gets home. Refer to yourself in the third person, and the child will soon catch on.

Some nannies feel guilt as well as a bit of pride and pleasure when this happens, and some may worry their job stability will be compromised by the situation. A rational employer who trusts your judgment will understand you would never try to confuse a vulnerable child about such a thing.

When the mothers—especially working mothers—find out, it's initially confusing to them, but then they develop strong feelings, whether jealousy, anger, or guilt for being out of the home. They question their skills as parents and whether they are doing a good enough job. Some mothers question whether it's the nanny's fault and if she's encouraging that behavior, and some will reprimand the nanny even when it's not warranted. Those parents' actions are fueled by the jealousy and guilt they feel, and they must try to avoid this trap, which may result in the loss of a caring caregiver who the child feels truly comfortable with.

There are even moms who change their nannies as often as possible to prevent their children from getting emotionally attached to the caregivers. What an absolutely ridiculous notion. When your child shows attachment to a nanny or calls her Mommy, feel secure you have done a good job in finding a compatible caregiver your child trusts and feels secure with.

To ease the minds of parents, what does research tell us about the tendency of children to call their caregivers Mommy and feel attached to them?

There's strong evidence babies and young children form strong emotional bonds with their caregivers, but they maintain the strongest attachments with their parents.

This stage is temporary, and kids grow out of it quickly. Below is some incredible research that will be reassuring to parents.

Reprinted with permission from the National Network for Child Care - NNCC.

What kinds of attachment are there?

The quality of attachment can be observed when the child greets the adult after an absence. If the infant approaches the adult, seems happy to see them, and is comforted by them, it is likely that a "secure attachment" exists. About three-fourths of infants have a secure attachment with their mothers by age 12 months.

The remaining one-fourth have insecure attachments—they are strongly attached, but the infant is not easily calmed or reassured by the adult. Some of them avoid the adult when she or he returns. Others give a mixed message—they go to the adult, then seem to resist being comforted. They may push off if held, or even cry as if angry.

Have you observed this? Childcare professionals verify with their own experience what researchers have observed in controlled experiments; infants form strong, secure attachments, not just to parents, but also to childcare providers. They also form secure attachments with other family members. In fact, some children even form something like an attachment with inanimate objects like their "security blankets".

Does the provider replace the parent? The short answer is "No." Researchers have investigated this possibility, and two of their research projects are worth describing in detail.

The kibbutz babies

Some agricultural communes (kibbutz) in Israel have used a form of day care that looks extreme by American standards. Group childcare begins at the age of four days, when the baby is brought home from the hospital. The baby sleeps and lives in an infant house under the care of a trained caregiver called a metapelet. The parents may see and care for the baby as much as they like. Typically the parents return to work within six weeks. By the time the infant is eighteen months old, most parents see the baby once each day for about three hours in the evening. The baby returns to the infant house to sleep.

The researchers asked: Will the infant be better able to use the metapelet or the mother to calm its fears? The investigators observed the infants using each adult to calm themselves after a stressful separation. The results showed that the infants were more secure with their mothers.

Given the small amount of time the mothers and their babies spent together, this was a somewhat surprising finding. We know that attachment is not a matter of biological bonding as it is with some other animals, for example, geese. Attachments are not formed immediately after birth but develop over time. For example, babies who are adopted early are no different from biological babies in their attachments to the parents who rear them.

So why did the babies have more effective attachments with their mothers on the kibbutz? Perhaps the mothers provided special attention to the infants. The metapelet, remember, had other infants to attend to during the day as well.

This idea is supported by research on American mothers who are employed full time outside the home. Many of them compensate for being away all day by giving their children extra attention in the evening. One study found that they spent as much time in high-quality interaction with their children each day as nonworking mothers did with their children.

An American experiment
With the growing number of infants in full-day care, American researchers have also wondered about childcare providers becoming like mothers to young children. In one study, each infant or toddler was videotaped in a somewhat stressful situation. To one side of the room was the child's mother and to the other side was the child's

provider. The adults were instructed not to talk or gesture to the child. Who would the child go to when stressed?

The results showed that the children spent much more time close to the mother than to the provider (and much more time close to the provider than to a stranger in the room). The infants were also most likely to share toys with, talk to, and touch their mothers. And they were more likely to do these things with their childcare provider than with a stranger.

The studies agree on two points. First, infants form secure attachments with their providers. Second, providers do not replace parents. The infant-parent attachment remains the most important emotional bond in the young child's life.

How does the child view this?
We began by noting that parents and providers alike are somewhat confused and embarrassed when a child calls the provider "Mommy." But how does the child feel?

Chances are good that the child doesn't know or care if you are embarrassed or jealous. From the child's point of view, all that matters is that he or she develops a secure attachment relationship in every important setting in his or her life. If this happens, then the child has a better chance of developing well socially, emotionally, and intellectually.

Clearly, parents and providers do not compete for the affection of young children. Providers are not substitute or alternate parents—they are supplementary caregivers. They supplement and support the efforts of parents to raise their children well.

If a child feels a trusting, secure, loving relationship with the childcare provider, parents should rejoice. Even if the child slips up and calls another adult "Mommy," the real mother can rest assured that she still has a special place in her child's life. She can be thankful that she has found a loving person in the community to help her raise her children.

References

Belsky, J., Lerner, R.M., & Spanier, B.G. (1984). The Child in the Family. Reading, MA: Addison-Wesley Publishing, pp. 37-58.

Farran, D.C., & Ramey, C.T. (1977). Infant day care and attachment behaviors toward mothers and teachers. Child Development, 48, 1112-1116.

Fown, N. (1977). Attachment of kibbutz infants to mother and metapelet. Child Development, 48, 1228-1239. http://www.nncc.org/Families/cc22_provider.like.mom.html[2]

---

[2] J. Belsky, R.M. Lerner, B.G.Spanier, "The Child in the Family," no. 37-58 (1984)

IT'S PERFECTLY OK TO SAY "NO" TO OVERTIME HOURS

A full-time job working with children for up to sixty hours a week is a demanding and difficult schedule. Not only are the workdays long for some nannies, but the multiple tasks to be completed during the day are physically demanding as well.

I once read the to-do list an employer gave her nanny, and I was flabbergasted. The demands were unrealistic in terms of the time needed to execute the tasks. The duties included cleaning the refrigerator, doing the laundry, and dusting the entire apartment thoroughly, ensuring every piece of furniture was moved and that space dusted as well. The above tasks were in addition to the childcare duties for a two-year-old child.

Situations like this are not uncommon. What's more shocking is even when the nannies have such daunting schedules, many employers insist the caregivers work on some evenings, weekends, and even holidays. The caregivers are compensated, but this does not make it right. They are not machines but everyday people who will get burned out with such an intense workload and need time to rest and recuperate after a demanding workweek.

While some of those caregivers welcome working extra hours, it's not acceptable when families get upset with caregivers who cannot fulfill their demands. Do the employers consider that most of these women have families and children of their own?

Families it's better to find a babysitter who will fill in on weekends and weeknights when you may need to take well deserved time off, rather than feeling frustrated when your current nanny isn't able to work overtime.

BE ORGANIZED, IT WILL MAKE CAREGIVING LESS STRESSFUL

Be organized! It will make caregiving less stressful. One key component of an effective childcare provider is great organizational skills. It is necessary in ensuring kids arrive at school and to playdates on time and so promises are met, and children don't miss their enrichment classes.

One way to help you juggle appointments is to use an appointment book or the calendar application on your phone. Sticky notes come in handy and can be posted on the refrigerator to serve as two-day reminders for appointments.

At the beginning of the school year, print out the children's school schedules and be aware of abbreviated school days, days off, and school breaks.

Scheduling and organizing are integral parts of juggling multiple kids' activities and playdates. This will save you the embarrassment of missing an early dismissal from school or an enrichment class.

"MY CHILD MATTERS"...NANNIES WHISPER THESE THREE WORDS EVERY DAY.

I'm left puzzled by the disrespect some parents show the children of the nannies who care for their kids every day. They act as though they are oblivious to the needs of the caregiver's children. They don't provide the caregivers with manageable schedules, so they have time to cook a meal for their children, help with their homework, or simply be there when they are sick. Some seem to forget the nannies have children of their own and insist they work long hours, weekends, and holidays.

Yet those same parents may be totally hands-on with their own kids and are involved in every aspect of their lives, including school, play, and social development. These are the parents who brag about their three-year-old's recital, enrichment class, or playdate, yet never ask the caregivers about their own children.

It's no wonder we live in an individualistic society where everyone seems absorbed in themselves. Parents model that behavior, and kids eventually emulate what they observe from their first teachers, the parents.

Does it not bother you that every conversation revolves around your life and circumstances? How do you think this makes the caregiver feel when she's not able to take time off to enjoy important milestones in her own child's life, like a first day at school, a graduation, an important doctor's visit, a play, and all the other events you never miss in your own child's life? This is such hypocrisy, because those employers indubitably love their children and should support another parent who wants to do same.

Does it not worry you that the caregiver may be unhappy that you never ask about her own precious kids? Perhaps that's the reason she seems inattentive and withdrawn from her job. Although I unequivocally disagree with the withdrawal behavior by some caregivers in situations like this, I understand why they may not feel motivated because of the selfish acts of their employers.

Nannies, when a family disregards your kids, especially young ones who may have similar needs as their children, initiate a conversation about how you feel. However, if you work for insensitive, irrational families, it might be time to look for a more humane family to work for.

If you don't show concern for your own children, don't expect your employer or anyone else to.

WHAT HAPPENS SOMETIMES AT SIX IN THE EVENING WHEN A PARENT TURNS THE KEY IN THE LOCK? MELTDOWN

It's six or seven in the evening and Mom or Dad turns the key to open the door, excited to see the kids. Within minutes, there is a complete uproar. Many sitters and nannies are nervous, because they do not want the parents to believe the kids have been upset all day, which is not usually the case.

Parents arrive home at a time when young kids are more prone to tantrums. They are getting sleepy and are exhausted from their day's busy schedule. Many young children have attended a full or partial day of school, enrichment classes, and playdates, and have explored parks and playgrounds, with limited time to nap. It's no surprise they act out.

Both parents and caregivers must remain calm. Kids will respond to the grown-ups' body language and reactions during those stressful situations. Make every effort to direct the child's attention to something else, like a favorite stuff animal or toy, or even make a funny face, to get them to giggle. Young children's attention span is limited and they are quick to turn their thoughts to something exciting. Also, ignore, as much as possible, situations that are not harmful to the child, such as whining. Continually telling the child to stop often encourages the unwanted behavior, as the child realizes it gets your attention.

These moments are powerful opportunities to reiterate to the children the need to effectively communicate their feelings verbally rather than crying. Although for sleepy children this may not make sense at the time, it ultimately teaches them to understand the need to use words.

Lastly, it's not a good time to punish. Change the atmosphere instead, with soft music, a favorite show, or an embrace and cuddle to help a tired child unwind.

GOING ON VACATION AND REFUSING TO PAY THE NANNY

How can a family book a vacation without taking into account the fact that the caregiver who works with the family needs to be paid? Some families arrange their annual vacation to coincide with the nannies' allotted vacation periods, but many outright refuse to compensate their caregivers when they are on vacation.

What is the norm? Families who value the services their caregivers provide and want to retain them will ensure that they are paid fully for whatever personal time the family takes. As long as the caregiver is not the one who disrupts the work schedule, she should be paid.

If the family and the caregiver have an agreement, however, where there will be no compensation during the family's vacation, then the caregiver who agreed to the work arrangements should not be upset when the situation occurs.

Caregivers need to carefully review what they are agreeing to during the hiring process, even if they are at a point of desperation when they think the need for a job outweighs the job description and compensation.

WORKING AFTER HOURS

Working extended hours as a caregiver is as common as wiping little tooshies and runny noses. Employers need extra time for date nights with spouses, for travel and business purposes. In most states, a family must be prepared to offer their caregiver a taxi allowance after eight at night, but there are many employers who are guilty of not respecting that rule and are inconsiderate about the caregiver's safety.

There are also many caregivers who take the train or bus at late hours, compromising their safety. This should be reviewed by the guilty families, and adjustments must be made.

For the caregivers who are given a taxi allowance but still trek on a bus or train with the goal of saving the additional money, remember that your safety and well-being supersede the extra dollars.

BE CONSISTENT WITH DISCIPLINE IN THE PRESENCE OR ABSENCE OF THE PARENTS

The key to discipline is consistency. Whatever parent-approved discipline method a caregiver uses has to be executed in the same way each time, whether or not the parents are present.

It's interesting to watch caregivers who use forceful tones and body language, and the kids respond immediately with the desired behavior. However, those caregivers may be unable to get the kids to respond positively to a directive when the parents are present. This tells me the caregiver lacks consistency with discipline, so the child does not take the caregiver seriously. Many caregivers will not use the strong, forceful tone they use in disciplining a child in the absence of the parent if the parent is now present. This confuses children, and many gravitate to the parents and avoid the caregiver altogether.

Children do not need to be shouted at in order to listen. What they need are people who understand their behavior and their reasons for acting out, as well as effective discipline measures that are consistent, no matter who is in the listening or viewing audience.

BE CONSIDERATE WHEN CHOOSING ENRICHMENT CLASSES FOR KIDS

Enrichment classes for children are powerful in nurturing social and developmental skills as well as increasing fine and gross motor skills through art, music, dance and so forth. However, a parent must be considerate when choosing those classes, especially if multiple children are involved.

Factor in the time the child leaves school, the commuting time, and the level of stress involved in the process for both the caregiver and the children.

So many parents choose classes right after the end of a child's school day and do not consider the time it takes to get to the class. When insufficient time is factored in, it becomes stressful, not only for the caregiver, but also the child. The rush involved in getting the child to the class, the time needed to change into the required attire, bathroom time, and simply time for the child to unwind must be considered when enrolling in an enrichment class.

PHRASES FROM NANNIES THAT MAKE ME SAY "OUCH" AND SHOULD NEVER BE USED

"I don't care what you want."
"I don't want to hear it."
"Because I said so."
"You are a bad child."
"Shut up."
"What's your damn problem?"
"You are such a brat."
"I'm going to leave you here and not come back."
"You are so stupid."
"You are so naughty."
"I'll lock you in this room if you don't stop crying."

Words are powerful nannies, and children remember the people who violated them and refused to listen to them or those who respected them and ultimately showed them kindness. What type of nanny would you love to be remembered for? *Help cultivate a harmonious and peaceful family environment for the kids you care for at all times.*

ABOUT THE AUTHOR

Alene Mathurin is a family/caregiver certified professional life coach and offers several different programs all geared to developing successful family-nanny relationship, ultimately creating a happy home for children. Her business website is www.yournannycoach.com. Her blog with focuses on constructive dialogue geared to educating both parents and caregivers can be accessed at www.mynannycircle.com. Parents can also utilize the job board on this website for placing help wanted advertisements for caregivers and finding resourceful information. Her online national nanny database, YoNanny, will be available for use in February, 2015. Below are some sample services Mathurin offers:

Programs Offered
1. **Nanny Coaching, Support, Mediation and Orientation**

Congratulations on hiring a nanny to care for your precious kids. I know it was in-depth, involved and at times a very daunting task. Great parents like you have taken all necessary precautions in ensuring you've hired the best possible candidate for your precious kids. As a former nanny, nanny agency owner, and a nanny and life coach for families, I know that the greatest challenges and anxieties for a nanny and family are within the first few months of employment and hence the reason to begin cultivating and promoting positive behaviors early, to avoid pitfalls later on. For this reason, I've created a program to support families as they transition the care of their kids from parent's role or either another nanny to a new caregiver.

2. **I.N.A.P. (Innovative Nanny Acclimation Program)**

Once the nanny is hired and introduced to your children it's imperative to immediately begin to develop a successful relationship with the nanny with every member of the family. Through the INAP initiative I will work with both the family and the nanny to acclimate the caregiver to every important aspect of the family dynamics, including parenting values, rules, home structure and every aspect of the family that defines them as a unit. An important aspect of this plan is being with the new nanny on the job location, the family's home, to transition this individual into the new role. This definitely reduces the anxiety of hiring a new person, since I become the eyes and ears for the parents for whatever duration of time they choose. This plan includes:
- An initial meeting with you and the nanny to understand both sides better and to understand your core value system
- A meeting with the family and kids to help understand the children better

- On the job location presence with the nanny to understand work ethics and skills and to provide reinforcement wherever needed
- On the job location presence to help ease the anxiety of parents who are nervous about allowing a new nanny to work with their kids
- Acting as a liaison between the nanny and the family
- Individual meeting with family and the nanny to get feedback from both sides
- Providing advice and support as needed to the family
- Personalized guidebook for the nanny, which details all pertinent information about the children, emergency contact information, crisis plans in the event of unforeseen situations like terrorist attacks, family routines, health related issues, and other in-depth information

3. Nanny and Family Mediation

Over the years I have seen nannies lose very good jobs and families lose very valuable nannies over situations that could have been worked on if they were effectively communicated. Sometimes it's as simple as understanding how cultural influences can hinder a nanny from communicating their true feelings that may ultimately affect job performance; or maybe the family is trying hard not to make the nanny uncomfortable, and in the process, avoiding communicating a problem. I can help you cultivate and enhance successful relationships with your nanny by starting or initiating that line of communication. I act as a mediator in cases where there may be workable conflict within the nanny-family relationship.

4. Nanny and family Networking Events

Have you attempted using one of the online nanny portals lately trying to search for the best caregiver for your family? Yes, it's very involved with hundreds of profiles to choose from with everyone showcasing the same set of skills. We know how daunting it is especially when you don't have too much time to spare. Join us for one of our monthly nanny-family networking events and meet either a great caregiver or a great family in person, in a relaxed cordial environment. Enjoy interview booths where you can have a private chat with a nanny who has piqued your interest. Use the expertise of the nanny coach to get as much information as needed. It's safe and allows you the ability to meet many candidates and a great chance to meet parents in your area who are also looking for nannies.

REFERENCES

Belsky, J., Lerner, R.M., & Spanier, B.G. "The Child in the Family." No. 37-58 (1984)

Farren, D.C.,< & Ramey, C.T. "Infant Day Care and Attachment Behaviors towards Mothers and Teacher." no.48, 1112-1116 (1977)

Weissbluth, M. Dr. "Healthy Sleep Habits, Happy Child." (1999)

Made in the USA
Middletown, DE
18 July 2015